The life and extraordinary history of the Chevalier John Taylor. Member of the most celebrated academies, ... Who has been on his travels upwards of thirty years, In two volumes. Volume 1 of 2

John Taylor

The life and extraordinary history of the Chevalier John Taylor. Member of the most celebrated academies, ... Who has been on his travels upwards of thirty years, ... Written from authentic materials, and published by his son, John Taylor, ... In two volu Volume 1 of 2

Taylor, John
ESTCID: T040926
Reproduction from British Library
Sometimes attributed to Henry Jones. Volumes continuously paginated.
Dublin : printed for D. Chamberlain, 1761.
2v.([2],iii,[1],162p.) ; 8°

Eighteenth Century
Collections Online
Print Editions

Gale ECCO Print Editions

Relive history with *Eighteenth Century Collections Online*, now available in print for the independent historian and collector. This series includes the most significant English-language and foreign-language works printed in Great Britain during the eighteenth century, and is organized in seven different subject areas including literature and language; medicine, science, and technology; and religion and philosophy. The collection also includes thousands of important works from the Americas.

The eighteenth century has been called "The Age of Enlightenment." It was a period of rapid advance in print culture and publishing, in world exploration, and in the rapid growth of science and technology – all of which had a profound impact on the political and cultural landscape. At the end of the century the American Revolution, French Revolution and Industrial Revolution, perhaps three of the most significant events in modern history, set in motion developments that eventually dominated world political, economic, and social life.

In a groundbreaking effort, Gale initiated a revolution of its own: digitization of epic proportions to preserve these invaluable works in the largest online archive of its kind. Contributions from major world libraries constitute over 175,000 original printed works. Scanned images of the actual pages, rather than transcriptions, recreate the works *as they first appeared.*

Now for the first time, these high-quality digital scans of original works are available via print-on-demand, making them readily accessible to libraries, students, independent scholars, and readers of all ages.

For our initial release we have created seven robust collections to form one the world's most comprehensive catalogs of 18th century works.

Initial Gale ECCO Print Editions collections include:

History and Geography

Rich in titles on English life and social history, this collection spans the world as it was known to eighteenth-century historians and explorers. Titles include a wealth of travel accounts and diaries, histories of nations from throughout the world, and maps and charts of a world that was still being discovered. Students of the War of American Independence will find fascinating accounts from the British side of conflict.

Social Science

Delve into what it was like to live during the eighteenth century by reading the first-hand accounts of everyday people, including city dwellers and farmers, businessmen and bankers, artisans and merchants, artists and their patrons, politicians and their constituents. Original texts make the American, French, and Industrial revolutions vividly contemporary.

Medicine, Science and Technology

Medical theory and practice of the 1700s developed rapidly, as is evidenced by the extensive collection, which includes descriptions of diseases, their conditions, and treatments. Books on science and technology, agriculture, military technology, natural philosophy, even cookbooks, are all contained here.

Literature and Language

Western literary study flows out of eighteenth-century works by Alexander Pope, Daniel Defoe, Henry Fielding, Frances Burney, Denis Diderot, Johann Gottfried Herder, Johann Wolfgang von Goethe, and others. Experience the birth of the modern novel, or compare the development of language using dictionaries and grammar discourses.

Religion and Philosophy

The Age of Enlightenment profoundly enriched religious and philosophical understanding and continues to influence present-day thinking. Works collected here include masterpieces by David Hume, Immanuel Kant, and Jean-Jacques Rousseau, as well as religious sermons and moral debates on the issues of the day, such as the slave trade. The Age of Reason saw conflict between Protestantism and Catholicism transformed into one between faith and logic -- a debate that continues in the twenty-first century.

Law and Reference

This collection reveals the history of English common law and Empire law in a vastly changing world of British expansion. Dominating the legal field is the *Commentaries of the Law of England* by Sir William Blackstone, which first appeared in 1765. Reference works such as almanacs and catalogues continue to educate us by revealing the day-to-day workings of society.

Fine Arts

The eighteenth-century fascination with Greek and Roman antiquity followed the systematic excavation of the ruins at Pompeii and Herculaneum in southern Italy; and after 1750 a neoclassical style dominated all artistic fields. The titles here trace developments in mostly English-language works on painting, sculpture, architecture, music, theater, and other disciplines. Instructional works on musical instruments, catalogs of art objects, comic operas, and more are also included.

The BiblioLife Network

This project was made possible in part by the BiblioLife Network (BLN), a project aimed at addressing some of the huge challenges facing book preservationists around the world. The BLN includes libraries, library networks, archives, subject matter experts, online communities and library service providers. We believe every book ever published should be available as a high-quality print reproduction; printed on-demand anywhere in the world. This insures the ongoing accessibility of the content and helps generate sustainable revenue for the libraries and organizations that work to preserve these important materials.

The following book is in the "public domain" and represents an authentic reproduction of the text as printed by the original publisher. While we have attempted to accurately maintain the integrity of the original work, there are sometimes problems with the original work or the micro-film from which the books were digitized. This can result in minor errors in reproduction. Possible imperfections include missing and blurred pages, poor pictures, markings and other reproduction issues beyond our control. Because this work is culturally important, we have made it available as part of our commitment to protecting, preserving, and promoting the world's literature.

GUIDE TO FOLD-OUTS MAPS and OVERSIZED IMAGES

The book you are reading was digitized from microfilm captured over the past thirty to forty years. Years after the creation of the original microfilm, the book was converted to digital files and made available in an online database.

In an online database, page images do not need to conform to the size restrictions found in a printed book. When converting these images back into a printed bound book, the page sizes are standardized in ways that maintain the detail of the original. For large images, such as fold-out maps, the original page image is split into two or more pages

Guidelines used to determine how to split the page image follows:

• Some images are split vertically; large images require vertical and horizontal splits.
• For horizontal splits, the content is split left to right.
• For vertical splits, the content is split from top to bottom.
• For both vertical and horizontal splits, the image is processed from top left to bottom right.

THE
L I F E

AND EXTRAORDINARY

H I S T O R Y

OF THE

Chevalier JOHN TAYLOR.

Member of the moſt celebrated Academies, Univerſities, and Societies of the Learned—Chevalier in ſeveral of the brſt Courts in the World—Illuſtrious (by Patent) in the Apartments of many of the greateſt Princes—Ophthalmiater Pontifical, Imperial and Royal—to His late Majeſty—to the Pontifical Court—to the Perſon of Her Imperial Majeſty—to the Kings of Poland, Denmark, Sweden, &c —to the ſeveral Electors of the Holy Empire—to the Royal Infant Duke of Parma—to the Prince of Saxe-Gotha, Sereniſſime Brother to her Royal Highneſs the Princeſs Dowager of Wales—to the Prince Royal of Poland—to the late Prince of Orange—to the preſent Princes of Bavaria, Modena, Lorrain, Brunſwick, Anſpach, Bareith, Leige, Salzbourg, Middlebourg, Heſſe caſſel, Holſtein, Zerbſt, Georgia, &c —Citizen of Rome, by a public Act in the Name of the Senate and People—Fellow of that College of Phyſicians—Profeſſor in Opticks—Doctor in Medicine and Doctor in Chirurgery in ſeveral Univerſities abroad

Who has been on his Travels upwards of thirty Years, with little or no Interruption, during which, he has not only been ſeveral Times in every Town in theſe Kingdoms, but in every Kingdom, Province, State, and City of the leaſt Conſideration—in every Court—preſented to every Crowned Head and Sovereign Prince in all Europe, without Exception. Containing the greateſt Variety of the moſt entertaining and intereſting Adventures, that, 'tis preſumed, has ever yet been publiſhed in any Country, or in any Language.

Written from Authentic MATERIALS, and publiſhed by his SON,
J O H N T A Y L O R, Oculiſt.

In TWO VOLUMES

D U B L I N:

Printed for D. CHAMBERLAIN in *Smock-Alley.*
M,DCC,LXI.

CONTENTS.

CHAP. V.

CHAP. VI.

CHAP. VII.

CHAP. VIII.

CHAP. IX.

CHAP.

CONTENTS. iii

CHAP. X.

CHAP. XI.

CHAP. XII.

CHAP. XIII.

CHAP. XIV.

CHAP. XV.

CONTENTS

OF THE

SECOND VOLUME.

THE

THE
LIFE
AND EXTRAORDINARY
HISTORY
OF
Dr. JOHN TAYLOR.

NATURE delights in the marvellous; the moral, as well as the phyſical World abounds with the Strange and Wonderful; every Country, nay, every Town, have their aditional Stories of this Kind, the very Villages boaſt their athletic Heroes, and their ruſtic Bards, which they compare and poize againſt each other with much Warmth and Emulation. That ſtiring *Proteus,* called Ambition, will act its Part in the human Soul under a thouſand different Marks. That reſtleſs Principle, which ſtimulates the Heart of Man, and goads it to aſpire; that Parent of every ſplendid Folly; that inborn Pride will work itſelf to View, and ſhine among the coarſeſt Rubbiſh.

Not *Cæſar,* in his higheſt Triumph, was more elated, than is poor *Hobbinol,* perhaps, at a Country Wake, to whom his fellow Ruſtics have yielded up the Prize for being the beſt Wreſtler, and breaking the moſt Heads: he gains the utmoſt Summit of his Wiſhes; he ſtands on high amongſt his Neighbours; a Garland, or a Hat, ſo purchaſed, are to him a little Kingdom. His Horizon, like that of his ſubject Cattle, is but narrow; and the Spot he feeds upon is all his Empire; yet even there he would triumph.

B

This

This energetic Fire, when it kindles up a daring Spirit, muſt look abroad, muſt ſtretch itſelf at large, and, like a Comet, travel through the vaſt Expanſe of Nature, viſit every Climate in its Courſe, amaze the learned in its ſwift Career, and ſcare the ignorant with idle Terrors, wondered at by all. Such Appearances are ſudden and un-looked for; they ſeldom come; and, when they do, all Nature ſeems too narrow for their Province; they ruſh with ſuch Rapidity to public View, and draw behind them a Train of Things the moſt extravagant and ſtrange, their Equipage of Character; where the grand and the ridiculous, the generous and the mean, the ſkillful and the rude, the good-natured and the baſe, the friendly and the perfidious, are all jumbled into one vaſt Coincidence of Extreams, that give Mankind an *Alexander*, perhaps, a *Charles* the Twelfth, a *Blood*, a *Creighton*, or a Chevalier *Taylor*, the matchleſs Hero of the enſuing Story, whoſe literal Exploits, founded upon Facts ſo manifeſt, ſo illuſtrious through all *Europe*, exceed, in Num-ber, and entertaining Incidents, the moſt fertile Romance, that Invention has hitherto produced; a Character ſo complex, and ſo contraſted, no Age, perhaps, or Country has beheld. It looks as if Nature, in a playful Frolic, had thrown him out to the World, in order to ſhew Mankind how Reaſon and Paſſion, how Genius and Ca-price, could counter-work each other within the human Mind, and mark out a moral Prodigy, made up of all Extremes.

Between the Hours of Eleven and One, on the Sixteenth Day of *Auguſt*, One Thouſand Seven Hundred and Three, did Nature and the Midwife give our matchleſs Hero to the World, the Sun and his Mother being in Labour at the ſame Time; he travelling through an Ecliple, and ſhe

in

in Travail of the illustrious Doctor, who at one Instant with the Sun, began to break out from Darkness, and, as the Parish Records testify, came into Light with him.

He no sooner began to distinguish Objects, than he expressed the greatest Aversion to all Spots, either upon the Garments, or Countenances of those to whom he came near. Patches, worn upon the Face, being then the Fashion, he often scratched them off, and sometimes brought the Blood along with them : nay, even then, he put some Eyes in Danger.

As he grew up he could not bear the least Spot upon Linen, China, or Spectacles in particular, which he often broke in his attempt to clean them. His Mathematical Master made him peep one Day at his Cotemporary, the Sun, through a good reflecting Telescope ; but the Spots he discovered there disturbed his Imagination to such a Degree, that it has been the Toil and Study of his whole Life to take them off, in order to which he has pursued him these Forty Years past, through all his Journeys, hoping to come up with him at one Stage or other, and there perform upon him an Operation, which would undoubtedly carry his Fame all round the World. But this, like some other points he pursues, seems to be a little beyond his Reach, but, to a Genius, nothing is impossible.

His Father was an honest Son of *Æsculapius*, a Man of Learning and Candour, in his Profession of Physick and Surgery ; but he dying before the present Doctor arrived at his Sixth Year, this Incident threw the Reins over our young Chevalier's Neck, and opened wide the Gate to all his future Glory.

His Mother was a careful, honest, good Kind of Woman ; she kept up the Business of an Apothe-

cary ;

cary; by which Means, fhe fupported our future Hero, with two other Children, in a very decent Manner.

The young Chevalier, after having fcrambled together fome fmall Matter of Learning, ftood as yet behind his Mother's Counter, in the Town of *Norwich*, where he had his Birth and Education. In this narrow Sphere of Action he remained fome Time unnoticed; but Obfcurity and he could not long keep Houfe together.

A rich old Quaker, within a few Doors of him was taken ill of the Cholic: Our young Artift is fummoned to his Relief; where *Tabitha*, the Quaker's new married Spoufe, happened to caft a favoury Leer at our handfome fpruce Doctor, than whom there was not a more comely Perfonage in all *Norfolk*. Lovers, like Angels, can talk by Intuition. A few kind Sentiments, exchanged in this filent, but emphatic Manner, foon opened the Congrefs to a more fubftantial Intercourfe. In a Word, the Doctor adminiftered to her in all Simplicity of Heart; and frequent were the Cordials of his Love: but, alas! no human Joy is certain. One fatal *Sunday* Morning, *Ebenezer*, who kept, it feems a feparate Bed, came haftily into his Wife's Apartment, with no other covering than his Shirt, being fuddenly ftirred, no Doubt, with the Spirit, of Propagation, and then, and there, furprized the happy guilty Couple; but the Doctor, in this infant Recounter, gave an early Specimen of that Addrefs and Dexterity, which have fo ftrongly marked the Character of all his future Adventures, he told the Quaker, with an Oath in his Mouth, and a Penknife in his Right Hand, that no Harm at all was intended by him, and that his Bufinefs there was only to cut his Wife's Corns: but the Quaker crying out Murder, the Doctor fprings

down

down Stairs at one Leap, takes ſhort Leave at Home, and ſcampers up to *London*.

CHAP. I.

The Reader, in the opening of this Character, will meet with the Embryo of our future Hiſtory, which will enlarge itſelf as we go on, and ſtretch out it's Parts to a prodigious Size.

OUR Chevalier now in the Nineteenth Year of his Age, arrives at the Capital, where he ſoon got behind another Apothecary's Counter, in *Cheapſide*; and, with his Peſtle, gave many loud preludes of his future Fame, which all *Europe* was one Day to hear. He rung his Mortar, that Prologue to a Paſſing-Bell, with ſuch Elegiac Notes, that ſeveral Neighbouring Undertakers, together with the Pariſh Sexton, would often aſk him to a Glaſs of Liquor, delighted with his Harmony; but a crabbed, ill-natured old rich Iron-monger, in the ſame Street, complained that his ears were torn to pieces by our Muſician's Noiſe, and threatened to have him ſilenced by Authority, but the ingenious and humane Doctor *Green* (his Maſter's Relation) took his Part againſt the Alderman, bid him go on, and called him his *Tubal Cain*; and being ſtruck by his lively Addreſs, together with his very comely Perſon, he told the young Spark, he would have his Picture done by *Kneller*, then the reigning Painter of *England*; for truly the young Doctor's Miſtreſs had a Mind to hang it in her Parlour, knowing the great Intimacy that was between Sir *Godfrey* and Doctor *Green*. *Kneller* had his Country Houſe at *Whitton*, a Place about fourteen Miles diſtance from Town. The Doctor carries young *Taylor* down thither; he ſits for his Picture, and diverts Sir *Godfrey* with his lively

B 3

Sallies

Sallies of Humour, which made such deep Impression on the Spirit of his Disciple Mr. *Richard Eagle*, commonly called *Dick Eagle*, a Name well known in all the Registers of Enterprise, that he invited our stripling Chevalier into a strict Friendship with him, and promised to put him quick into a Capacity to spurn at an Apothecary's Shop

The Doctor thanked him, and returned to Town, where he again regaled the Neighbourhood with his Melody, and went on in the same musical Manner about a Fortnight longer; but being sent one Day by his Master to visit a Patient as far off as *Bridges Street, Covent Garden*, at his Return thro' *Vinegar Yard*, into *Drury Lane*, he was accosted out of a Garret Window by his worthy Friend Mr. *Richard Eagle*, who, calling him by his Name, asked him to come up Stairs, for he had something to tell him: Up he goes; and there he found with his Friend Mr *Eagle*, a grey-headed gaudy-dressed old Gentleman, in Company with a flustered Bawd, and two ragged Bunters, each of whom had a black Eye.

There stood upon a Stool a full Bowl of Punch, *Dick Eagle*, at his entering the Room, whispered something in the old Gentleman's Ear, who immediately drank to the Doctor, shook him by the Hand, nay, squeezed it in a very particular Manner.

Dick Eagle began a Song, or rather a kind of Interlude, called *Roger came tapping at Dolly's Window*, which he acted with much Humour and Address. He set the Doctor and the old Gentleman a laughing very heartily. The Bawd and her Pupils were now vanished. *Dick* put the Glass about with some Vigour: he filled lustily to the young *Hippocrates*, who, not being accustomed to deep Drinking, found himself strangely exhilarated;

rated; and taking *Dick* by the Hand, in the Honefty of his Heart, called him his Friend, and what would he not do to ferve him?

Dick drank his Health in a Bumper; and nodding at the old Letcher, flipt down Stairs, leaving the young *Æfculapius* and Sir *Francis* together, who, fitting clofer to the Stripling, put into his Hand a Purfe, with Gold in it, which he begged him to accept of, as a Mark of his Regard for him; and then proceeded to fome Singularities, which alarmed our young Chevalier ftrangely; who could by no Means guefs at his Defign: but the old Villain becoming ftill more and more explicit, the Doctor, in a Rage, called him Scoundrel, knocked him and the Stool, Punch Bowl and all to the Floor, which made fuch an Earthquake, that it foon brought *Dick*, the Bawd, and her Pupils, into the Room, who in great Dudgeon afked, if he was going to rob the Gentleman.——

Our hot Hero drawing the old Man's Sword, drove the Wenches out again, and in the Scuffle wounded *Dick* in the Leg: then bouncing down Stairs into the Street, with a bloody Sword waving in his Hand, he fcampered along *Drury Lane*, leaving his Hat, Wig, three fmall Vials, and a large Clyfter Bag behind him.

The People thought him mad. In his Way he encountered the worfhipful Mr. Juftice *Vaughan*, who lived then in *Bow Street, Covent Garden*. He ftops and difarms our frighted Fugitive, afked him with much Earneftnefs, what was the Matter?

Young *Taylor* related to him at large the whole Affair, which he did with fuch Colourings of Truth and Honefty, that the fenfible Juftice made no Scruple of going back with him to the very Spot where the Thing happened; and promifed him all the Redrefs imaginable.

So back they marched, the Justice now bearing the bloody Sword in one Hand, and the frighted Youngster in the other, followed by Curiosity in the Shape of a gaping Multitude.

They are now arrived in *Vinegar Yard* : the Justice mounts first, the Doctor at his Heels ; his Worship entered the Garret, like a broken-winded Jade, puffing and blowing, and holding both his Sides. He no sooner saw the old Son of *Sodom*, who had by this Time, stuck a Piece of brown Paper, steeped in Vinegar, to his Eye, than he cryed out, as fast as Breath would give him Leave, Fye, Shame, Sir *Francis*, now I am sure the Lad spoke Truth—a Man of your Years—but the Law shall —and you, you pimping ignominious Rascal, for such a rancid old Goat, and Girls onoo, shocking Scoundrel ! Go fetch a Constable. Your Leg, you Pander, I wish it was your Guts—O Scandal ! an innocent Country Lad ! your Money shall not save you, Sir *Francis*.

The Barber was busy now about *Dick Eagle*'s Wound, but, hearing of Law and Constables, he left his Patient in a Panic, who bled so fast, that the Justice ordered a Surgeon to be sent for ; and, leaving a Guard over *Dick*, he sent Sir *Francis*, and the Bawd with her three Pupils, to the Gatehouse ; then calling a Coach, he put the young *Celsus* into it, who had, by this Time, gathered up his Hat and Wig, Clyster Pipe, and Bottles ; the Purse *Dick Eagle* had secured.

The good Justice set him down at his Master's Door, in *Cheapside*, to whom he related the whole Matter, and told him, that the Lad must certainly prosecute them.

Mr. *Brady* thanked his Worship very kindly, and said, the Boy should attend him when and where he pleased.

The

The Juſtice took his Leave; and young *Tubal* began again to ring his Mortar.

His Miſtreſs was much alarmed, and took on mightily: it was to be ſure a vaſt Misfortune to be handſome,—the Monſter did not hurt him,—ſhocking Wretches!——ſhe'd ſee them get to *Tyburn*,—*Jack* was handſome to be ſure,——Aye, he ſhould ſwear——Here, take this Glaſs of Sack——Come, drink it up——Lord! how I tremble!—Oh! the filthy Monſter! Here, take another I tremble ſo ——he did not hurt you, *Jack*,——I am all I don't know how,——My Hand,——Come, *Jack*, here's your Health,——Feel me, how I ſhake with Anger.

Jack was not ſo dull, but he ſoon ſaw that all this was leading to a certain Explanation; but People calling in the Shop, he made his Bow, and got behind the Counter. His kind Miſtreſs ſtill followed him with her Pity, and curſed Sir *Francis* from her Heart.

Mr *Brady*, being an able Surgeon, as well as Apothecary, ſpared no Coſt to procure Subjects for Diſſection. He often trafficked at *Tyburn* for Bodies, which he uſed to place at his Table, like living Gueſts, in order, no doubt, to make ſuch Objects familiar to his Pupils, who are apt to be ſtartled at the appearance of dead Bodies.

The firſt of theſe Gentry, to whom our freſh Man was introduced, put him into ſuch a Fright, that he ſtarted, turned pale, and a cold Sweat hung upon his Forehead, which his kind Miſtreſs wiped off with great Tenderneſs, and ſaid, her Huſband was a barbarous Man, for frighting the poor Youth in ſuch a cruel Manner.

So he grew worſe, was put to Bed, his Miſtreſs followed him, and, by one kind means or other, brought him to himſelf again How he returned his Acknowledgments at that Time, is, we confeſs a little in the dark ; but her Countenance, at coming down, expreſſed no Marks of Diſappointment.

He ſoon ſcraped an Acquaintance with theſe Culprits defunct, and made a happy Progreſs in the Study of Anatomy ; he grew fond of it to a Degree, and often went, with his Maſter and Fellow Pupils, to dig up Bodies, in the neighbouring Church-Yards, at Midnight.

In one of theſe Excurſions, it ſeems, that ſome Friends of the Party interred had Notice of their Deſign, and waited to prevent them. The Perſon, whoſe Remains were that Day committed to the Earth, happened to be a ſwaggering *Iriſh* Beaux, who dyed, for the Good of his Country, at a noted Place near *Paddington.*

Half a dozen luſty Boys of the Sodd were determined that he ſhould keep his Lodgings unmoleſted, until he had a lawful Summons to get up, and march off with the reſt of his Neighbours They ſwore it was a cruel Caſe that a Man ſhould be torn out of his Grave, and ſcattered about the World, from Place to Place, in ſuch an unchriſtian Manner ; it was a Breach of Hoſpitality, which the living never met with in *Ireland,* let alone the dead ; and, by Heaven, *Shillaly* * ſhould try Titles for it.

One of them, being a Prieſt, obſerved, that the Atoms of *Phelim O' Byrn* would, by that Means, be diſperſed throughout the Univerſe, and loſt in the common Maſs of Matter ; or, what is ſtill worſe, ſays he, his Catholick Clay may chance to be mixed with Heretic Mortar, and help to build up ſome damned Preſbyterian Meeting Houſe, which, by *Jeſus,* would grieve his very Heart in

---

* A Cant Word, in *Ireland,* for an Oak Sapling, from a Wood there of that Name.

Purgatory

Purgatory: Confider, fays he, at the Day of Judgment, when People will be all in fuch a Hurry, and every one ftriving to be foremoft, before poor *Phelim* can gather himfelf up again, half the World will get to Mount *Calvary*, and *Phelim*, perhaps, may be punifhed for Contempt of Court; fo that it is, Gentlemen, a Principle of Confcience, as well as Honour, to defend his Remains from thefe nocturnal Vultures: And fo to Work they went, and laid about them luftily, Prieft and all.

The Mafter Surgeon left, upon the Field of Battle, his Cane, his Hat, his Great Coat, and his Sword; the reft of his Band were difperfed feveral Ways, and hotly purfued by fix ftout *Shillaly* Plants, which, as Father *Tedy* obferved, had then no Time to grow idle.

Our young Chevalier, being by much the moft active of his Troop, took to his Heels, with the lofs of all his upper Garments, except a Waiftcoat without Sleeves: his Head Cloaths were miffing, which Retrenchments helped to make him vifible, in a Summer's Dawn, at fome Diftance. He flew to a Houfe, upon a Hill Side, about half a Mile to the North Eaft of *Pancrafs* Church Yard, for that was the Field of Battle. He was attracted thither by a Light he faw in one of the Windows, though it was then about Two o'Clock in the Morning.

To the Door he came, and, with all the Pathos of Impatience and Fear, begged, for Pity's Sake, to be admitted; fwore he was purfued by Robbers, who had ftripped, and abufed, and now were going to murder him.

A Cafement opened, and a foft Voice afked him, Who, and What he was. He repeated his Story and Intreaties, with fo much Energy and Perfuafion,

that

that they, with his beautiful Person, soon prevailed upon the Door to unlock.

In he went and there he found half a Dozen jolly Fellows sitting round the Remains of an almost expiring Bowl of Punch, a Libation to *Hymen*; for, truly, there was a Wedding. They all stare at the half naked Doctor: He repeats his Tale, with Terror in his Eyes.

Scarce had he finished, when a dreadful Thunder, with loud Oaths and Menaces, was battering at the Door. He crys for Pity's sake to hide him in the Oven, under the Brewing Pan, or any where; when, lo! a good-natured elderly Gentlewoman in her Night-Gown only, opens gently a Parlour Door, who, seeing the sweet Countenance and genteel Shape of the distressed Petitioner, she said, with Tenderness, ' Come, come here, Child, I'll hide ' you safe ; the Rogue, shan't find you here.' So saying, she took him by the Hand, and led him to an inner Room : She made him creep under a Bed, and bid him not stir for his Life, till she should call him.

By this Time the cannonical Captain and his Troop were entered, and demanded the sacrilegious Villain, who had taken Shelter here.

The Centinels, doing Duty at the Bowl, were too far gone to dispute the Matter, so yielded at Discretion ; yet still denying that any such Person was under that Roof.

The good Gentlewoman begged to know what the Matter was ; upon which the Priest, Father *Tedy* by Name, gave them a short, but full Account of the whole Business. Said he was sorry to disturb any Neighbours at their Merriment ; ' but, says ' he, a Crime of this Nature, I think, should be ' severely punished.'

' Is

' Is that all, cries one of the nocturnal Soakers ?
' If the Dead only have Cause of Complaint in
' this Matter, the Affair, I believe, must lie over a
' few Terms longer : It is certainly the Business of
' a foreign Jurisdiction ; and at the Day of Judg-
' ment, and not before, the Parties shall have a fair
' Hearing. In the man Time, fill up the Bowl,
' and let us drown all Animosity.'

So said, so done, Father *Tedy* and his Friends
began to quench their Resentments apace : they
listened to Reason with a pure good Will ; but one
of them, a Kinsman it seems of the deceased *Phelim
O'Byrne*, began to weep at the Remembrance of
their former Friendships and Adventures. Upon
which Father *Tedy* commanded him to refrain,
adding, at the same Time, that nothing was so *eki-
vocal* as a Tear ; inasmuch, says he, as it may pro-
ceed from the Extremity of the different Affections
of either Grief or Joy. St. *Cyprian* has it, *La-
chryma*, &c.

The antient Lady entered heartily into the Con-
troversy of the Glass, and recommended Unity and
Good Will. She said, it was Pity so handsome a
young Gentleman as they denied Quarters to,
should meddle in such odd Frolicks : but, added
she, perhaps he is some Surgeon's Prentice, and
thinks he was doing no more than his Duty. She
was sorry they refused him Admission.

Why really, says Father *Tedy*, if that be the
Case, I should not be against receiving him upon
Terms of Penance, since it is from the Intention
only that we are to form an Estimate of the moral
Good or Evil of any human Act, the Intention is
every thing, and the Agent is no more than a mere
Machine in the Case. The Intention is every thing,
Gentlemen.

No, Sir, answered a Person in a Grazier's Coat,
who sat like *Hogarth*'s Priest, predominant at the
Bowl,

Bowl, there is something more wanting to make up one of your Sacraments. Due Form, due Matter as well as requisite Intention: for, I find, you are one of the Pope's recruiting Serjeants here in *England*; and let me tell you, Sir,———

Here the antient Lady once more broke in, and begged that no difference about Religion or Politicks should hinder her bringing the young Gentleman into Company, provided it were agreeable to the Majority. To which Father *Tedy*, willing to drop the Subject readily agreed; and answered for himself and Companions, saying, Madam, if the Gentleman be really here, pray introduce him immediately; it will be very pleasing to us all.

Up sprung Dame *Kitely*; and with a joyful Voice, cried out, Come, Culprit, come from your Hole, you Rogue you: what asleep! where are you, ha? neither in the Bed, nor under it?——By the Lord, Gentlemen, he is gone, and what is still worse, the Bride is gone too: aye, here the Sash stands open; was ever such an accident! O Mr. *Milksop*, your Bride is gone · what will your Mother say?—— Sure no Harm is done! For Heaven's Sake, Gentlemen, get up and pursue, and bring back this gigling silly Girl. No Harm, I hope, has happened.

At this the whole Company, Bridegroom, Priest, Parson, and all were in the Fields in a Moment; but, alas! the Scent by this Time was quite cold; and Half the Pack at least were not only at a Loss, but lost themselves; some staring, some reeling, some gaping between Wonder and Surprise, not knowing what to say or do, others were busy about the Bridegroom, who had tumbled into a Ditch, half choaked with Mudd and Filth; where we will leave Father *Tedy* and the Parson busy to tugg and pull him out, and follow the Bride and young Chevalier, who had got, by this Time, as

fat

far as *Gray's-Inn-Lane*; he in his Waistcoat, as before, without Headcloaths, and Miss *Jenny* in her Gown and Under Peticoat, where the Watch, in their Hospitality, made Provision for them in the next Round-house.

Here the stripling Knight Errant encountered his old Friend *Dick Eagle*, who was his Senior in that Academy, two whole Hours at least, and was led in, like him, with a Lady under his Protection, whom he had purloined that very Evening from her Husband, a Man of Credit and Consequence in the Town of *Kingston upon Thames*.

It seems he, *Richard Eagle* by Name, had prevailed upon her to borrow from her Husband, without his Knowledge or Consent, some few Trinkets of Value, which, together with her Person, amounted to a certain Charge well known at the *Old Baily*, by the Name of Felony.

The Doctor no sooner saw *Dick*, than he cryed out, Hah, you Scoundrel, have I met you here at last? Is this your *Roger came tapping*, your gouty Sir *Francis*, you pimping Son of a Whore: a common Pimp is a Prince to you, you Whipper in of *Sodom*. I have heard enough of you, you Rascal.

Hear me, hear me, dear *Jack*, says *Dick*, the Fortune was the Thing I had in view. What, replied the Doctor, on such damned Conditions?—— O you Scoundrel, how like a Thief you look? To which *Dick* answered, If we may judge from Appearances, Sir, your Aspect is not the most Orthodox in the World. Pray, Sir, why so disincumbered: where's your Tunick, your Quoif and Castor: methinks the Lady too was a little in Haste; her Drapery is but thin; mere Gauze indeed. The Climate is warm. I warrant you your whole Contour is somewhat questionable. Pray

tell

tell the Conſtable and the Jury what you know of this Matter.

With that the Company burſt into a loud Laugh, and offered the Lady a Glaſs of Gin to comfort her, which ſhe kindly accepted of.

Oh, oh, ſays *Dick*, I ſee that Miſs is, indeed, a Whore, and the young Doctor her————

What, you Raſcal, anſwered *Jack*, is your Leg got well again? Then knocking up his Heels with great Dexterity, down comes *Dick* at his full Length whap upon the Floor. His Length was not extraordinary; ſo ſpringing up very nimble, a Battle enſued, where ſucceſs hung doubtful; for *Dapper Dick*, though not near as tall as his Antagoniſt, had the Advantage of a good Education at *Hockley in the Hole*, and managed his Knuckles with ſuch Dexterity, that the young Doctor had near enough on't.

But now the Prince of Darkneſs proclaimed a Peace, which, with ſome Reluctance, was at laſt obeyed.

The Conſtable then deſired the Doctor to give a ſhort, but true Account of his Adventure, which, indeed, he did, from the Beginning, with great Exactneſs.

But, ſays the Conſtable, how came you to preſs the Lady into the Service, with ſuch Precipitation?

Jack anſwered, I was no ſooner got under the Bed, than I heard ſomething ſtir upon it, and a Voice at the ſame Time, which uttered theſe Words; Damn me, what Frolick is this, to put the Booby under the Bed; I think Mrs. *Giſſon* is got into her Tantrams: then, ſtretching out her Hand, My Dear, ſays ſhe, come into Bed; there's enough of theſe Frolicks: leave the drunken Sots together. I muſt confeſs my Fears gave way; I could not reſiſt ſo kind a Call.

Miſs

Miſs ſoon found her Miſtake; and Things were now ſo far gone, that there was no Remedy but going on farther.

In ſhort, Matters went ſo well, that ſhe agreed to get out at Window with me, and leave the Milkſop her Huſband to wear the Willow, and be damned. It was a Match of Mrs. *Gibſon*'s making, for Ends of her own. She did not care if the Devil had the Prieſt, and the Bridegroom too. Mrs. *Gibſon*, ſhe ſaid, lived at the lower End of *Little Queen Street*; kept an Academy, and ſhe was one of her Pupils; but meeting with an Accident, in the way of Buſineſs, ſhe retired to Mr. *Milkſop*'s for her Health; where he thought proper, truly, to fall in love with her; which tender Paſſion of his through Mother *Gibſon*'s Aſſiſtance, ſoon ripened into Matrimony; but ſhe liked me much better for a few Nights than him. She did not care if the Devil had them all. Here ſtands the Lady, let her deny it if ſhe can.

Not I, by Heavens, ſays Miſs *Jenny*; but I wiſh I had my Cloaths again.

By this Time his worthy Friend Dr. *Green* was arrived; for *Jack* had ſent him Notice how Matters ſtood. The Doctor ſoon ſettled with the Conſtable; equipped the Chevalier with ſome Covering; Miſs *Jenny* was taken Care of for the preſent; *Dick Eagle* and his Damſel were ſent to *Newgate* for further Examination; and ſo the Court broke up for this Time.

CHAP.

CHAP. II.

In this Chapter an Incident of a striking Complexion begins to lay open and explain the Text of our intended Narrative. The Reader will quickly see more of it.

OUR Doctor went on in the Improvement of his Pestle and fine Person. The Harmony of the one, the Appearance and Address of the other were audibly and visibly in the Increase. He now began to look down upon the Undertakers and Sexton, the Parson himself vouchsafes to be his Acquaintance, and often asked him to his House, nay even the rigid unmusical Ironmonger began to soften his Severity ; and, by the Help of a little black Wool stuffed into his Ears, our loud sounding *Syren* had by Degrees less and less Influence over his litigious Temper, till at last he could (as the saying is) sleep like the Smith's Dog under the Anvil, nay snore after Dinner, though then the medical Peal was in its highest Paroxysm.

But Chance, or Fortune, or Luck, or what you please to call it, would not suffer this *Fiat Lux* to be longer shut in from the world. He had, like his Brother the Sun, his Race to finish, and a gigantic Race it was indeed.

It often happens, that the smallest Springs give Motion to the largest Bodies, the slightest Causes bring the greatest Effects to Birth.

Lo ! Miss *Jenny*, among the Multitude of her Experiments, could not forget some certain agreeable Incidents which happened on her Wedding-Night near *Pancrass*; they were working in her Memory every now and then ; and sometimes they struck the Organs of her Fancy.

Ac

As all Excellence is founded in Relation, and
Things are good and bad merely from Comparison,
she could not but give the Preference where it was
certainly due: And *Jenny* thought herself a Judge;
yea, she was frequent in her Visitation to the young
Chevalier, but not in *propria Persona*; no, she
came accoutred in his own Coat, Hat, and Breetches;
the two first of these Father *Tedy* had bestowed
on Mrs. *Gibson* as Trophies of the Field near *Pancrass*, the other under Articles were supplied by
Jack himself, in order to carry on his amorous
Project.   She came as a young Spark, who stood
in need of the Doctor's Help in certain Parts of his
Profession.   The Docter administered.   The Cure
went on as a Palliative only, for the Patient often
relapsed.

  Jack's Mistress, about this Time, began to take
sharp Notice of his Doings.   She watched him
close, and thought she spyed something odd in the
Behaviour of his Friend and Patient, something
that sent her Fancy back a roving to *Vinegar-
Yard*.

  Sir *Francis*, *Dick Eagle*, and the Lord knows
what, *Jack*, and his Patient, used to go up into a
back Room two pair of Stairs high, in order to
examine and compare Things together.   Where,
one unlucky Day, the Devil, in the Shape of Curiosity, prompted the Houshold-Dove to follow up,
and peep through a Chink.   What was her Asto-
nishment? she screamed, she clapped her Hands,
she cried out, The Villain *Dick Eagle* hath undone
him——Oh Husband! Husband! your House is
cursed——Mr. *Brady*, *Sodom* and *Gomorrah*——O
you smock-faced Villain! Such a hellish Prank, and
I at Home too! Oh *Jack, Jack!*——But *Newgate*
shall——

                                      Her

Her Hufband now came running up, Why, what the Devil Madam's here ? You'll frighten all the Parifh !

O the filthy Creatures, Hufband ! What a pocky Cafe !—a Fiftula perhaps —

The Devil's in the Woman. Is the Houfe on Fire ? What's the Matter, *Jack?*

I'll tell you, Sir, fays *Jack*, and fpringing, at one Leap, he cleared the half Pace, then down he ran, and in a Moment reached the Street, leaving poor *Jenny* in her Mafquerade, to act her Part as well as fhe could. He had an Uncle at *Hoxton*, near *Moorfields*, who lives in the fame Spot to this Hour : To him he ran and told his Story.

Mifs *Jenny*, in the mean while, was on her Trial. Mrs. *Brady*'s Evidence was point blank. The Judge was going to pafs Sentence, but *Jenny* begged a Moment's Refpite, defired to fpeak a Word in private with Mrs. *Brady*, where fhe foon difcovered the naked Truth. She is fent to *Tottle-fields* to take the Air ; where fhe ruminates fadly over the Hempen Block, and curfes from her Heart her nuptial Night near *Pancrafs*.

CHAP. III.

Matters now begin to grow ferious, and put on an Air of Confequence The Story begins to look like Bufinefs. But let us go on.

OUR Doctor is kindly received by his Uncle, who advifed him of all Things to return to his Mafter.

No, fays the Chevalier, that can never be. I feel my Heart enlarge itfelf. Something tells me, Uncle, that I fhall, one Day, make the World admire me. I'll ring no more the Mortar. I

have

have another Part to act. Affist me to appear in proper Colours. A Fortune I shall make, Sir. The Ladies will obferve this Shape and Perfon. A Mien like mine to ftand behind a Counter!

In fhort, his Uncle equipt him in the Habiliments of a young Phyfician, juft going to open the Campaign; a large ty'd Periwig, a Suit of Sables, Scarlet Cloak, Cane and Sword, &c. &c.

With thefe medical *Infignia*, and his fine Perfon, now in the Bloom of Youth and Spirits, out he fallies and feels a fecret Pride exulting at his Heart; his Pulfe beats high ——— a Fortune; a Coach and Six were ever prefent to his Fancy. Another *Quixot* with as warm a Frenzy, but a much more pleafing Countenance.

He had not long purfued his Adventures, before he was ftruck by an agreeable young Lady, who had, it feems, more Merit than Fortune.

Love is the firft and moft powerful of all Beings, Ambition, Avarice, and the reft are but Lackqueys in his Train.

The Doctor pays him Homage. The Match is made at Blind-man's buff, and he is married. But, alas! the Honey Moon is melted down—his Fever is abated—he begins to ftare about, and wonders where he is. He finds out, by Degrees, that a little Cafh might have made his Yoke much more agreeable : But that was too vulgar an Enquiry for him before Marriage, and was, now alas! a fruitlefs one after it.

He had got into Debt a good deal, and had no Wife's Portion to pay it with. His Mother however fupplies him with feveral Sums, from Time to Time. But fhe foon found that the Doctor could fpend more Thoufands than fhe had Twentys: Notwithftanding fhe let him have one Sum more; the laft he was ever to expect from her. She gave him thirty Guineas to open his Way into St.

Thomas's

Thomas's Hofpital as a young Surgeon, where that excellent Artift Mr. *Chefelden* then prefided; from whom Chevalier *Taylor* received the firft Rudiments of his Art as an Oculift, and to whom he was afterwards an Honour.

Being now come to Age, he took Poffeffion of his Manfion-Houfe, as he called it; but to his great Surprize, he found it mortgaged by his Mother, in order to defray the Charges of his Education. He fells it for two hundred Pounds, promifes his Mother her Moiety of that Sum; which, thro' Hurry or Inadvertence, he forgot to perform. And, in his great Generofity, he gave his younger Brother a Shilling.

A fine Shop is now preparing at *Norwich*. Drugs are fent for from *London*, with an Apparatus for cutting for the Stone; Midwifery, &c. &c. Fine Furniture was not forgot. But, before the elegant Doctor could open in form, he was attended with more Creditors than Patients. Cutting for the Stone he foon laid down, as his firft Attempt in that Way proved unfuccefsful, though the Procefs was allowed by good judges to be well purfued.

The Doctor as yet unhackny'd in the Ways of Men, had great Regard to his moral and profeffional Characters, notwithftanding a few family Slips. Midwifery he had not long purfued, having it feems, a greater Propenfity to make pregnant than to bring forth; as the firft Operation, he faid, was abfolutely neceffary to multiply the Species; whereas, in the other Cafe, Nature often did her own Bufinefs, without any Affiftance from Art.

Though the Doctor had, at this Time under his Tuition, feveral genteel Pupils, who brought him in a round Sum; yet his profufe Way of Living, in lefs than fix Months, drove him into Sanctuary, where he remained, till his Creditors could be pre-

vailed

vailed upon to fign a certain Inftrument, called a Letter of Licenfe.

During his Retirement, he got, by way of Amufement, two Wenches with Child, while his Wife was bufy abroad in conciliating his Creditors. One of the Girls was brought to-bed about a Fortnight before the other; when he found it no fmall Difficulty to give Security to the Parifh-Officers. He perfuaded the other, after her Lying-in, being now upon the verge of a Decampment, to put on Boy's Cloaths, attend him as his Page, and fly off with him to *Holland*; which fhe did. But an Accident there difcovered her Sex, which obliged the Doctor to fend her packing Home again, the Laws in *Holland* being very fevere againft fuch Mafqueradings.

The Doctor however, broke the Ice, (as the Saying is) in this Country with fome Succefs. He reftored to Sight the Daughter of a rich *Jew*, which the Faculty had given up as incurable; for which Exploit he was very well rewarded by her Father. But the Doctor thought himfelf in Gratitude obliged to do fomething more for his Money. He laboured to clear up the Eye of her Mind, and by many feeling Arguments put ftrongly home to her, and preffed upon her, was making her a Convert to Chriftianity as faft as he could. But the Doctor's Zeal happened to be a little indifcreet: For the young Lady's Aunt overheard his Cafuifty one Day as fhe went up Stairs, through the Means of a loquacious Bedfted; and being herfelf a *Hebrew* of the *Hebrews,* a Daughter of *Abraham* in the right Line, fhe foon apprized the *Canaanite* her Brother, what kind of Miffionary he had got into his Family.

Alarmed at the News, Old *Shylock* was for putting him to Death immediately. But his Wife, much more inclined to Mercy than he, oppofed it

by

by all Means, and advifed to keep him in clofe Confinement, till an Opportunity of fending him abroad to the *Eaft Indies* fhould happen, which muft foon be, as feveral Ships were getting ready to fail in a few Days for that Country; and then, fays fhe, he may be difpofed of, without any Danger to us, or our Daughter's Reputation: To which Propofal, *Shylock*, after fome Difficulty, agreed; but added he, the Villain fhall take *Abdes* every Day he ftays here.

Now, whether the above Advice, given by the Wife, proceeded from Prudence, Pity, or any other moral or human Principle, is, perhaps with the Doctor himfelf, no fmall Matter of Doubt, fince, by fpelling and putting Things together, he has Reafon to fufpect that certain Motives of quite a different Complexion were the real Caufe. But, be that as it may, our Occulift is now in the Dark himfelf, clofely confined, where he fed upon the Bread of Affliction, and drank the Water of Bitternefs for three whole Days together. On the fourth he faw Light, which, as *Milton* fays, ferved only to difcover Sights of Woe.

Lo! now three Olive-coloured, ugly Ruffians entered his Dungeon, with rueful Looks, and with Lamps in their Hands. They lead him down a back Stair-cafe, into a deep and difmal Cellar, where he faw the angry *Jew*, his Wife and Sifter. He faw and trembled. When lo! a large capacious Copper Ciftern ftands ready to receive him. Thither the three Ruffians led him. Naked, as he was, except about the middle, where fomething like *Adam's* Figg-leaf did him the like Office, in they hove him, and turned at once upon him twenty Cocks; which, like the Cataracts of *Nile*, came rufhing from above, below, and round about him.

Now, fays the *Jew*, thou vile *Nazarene!* pump or drown.————There was a Pump, and, with
Emulation

Emulation great as *Hercules*, the Doctor feized it. He labours now for Life—he counterworks the Cocks.—He cries aloud for Mercy : But *Shylock* told him if he loved Baptifm, he had now Water enough to wafh away his foul Pollutions. —He toils, and is a Match for all the Currents. And now the Smoke, like *Ætna's* reeking Top, afcends in Volumes from his Forehead. He keeps for once a Medium. His Comings-in and Goings-out are nearly equal, it could not laft—the Ballance now is turned. How unlike his Coffers ! A Plethory prevails, and he is oppreffed by Fulnefs—the Water rifes as his Sinews flacken—they mount triumphant to his Neck. Ah ! there, fays *Shylock*, fhould a Halter lodge. They reach his Chin.

And now the Wife cries out for Mercy. The Doctor is reprieved—they lay him at his length—they give him Breathing-time—they give him Gin —he rifes—they lead him to his difmal Manfion. Three Days he underwent this watery Purgatory.

The fourth, at Noon, his Crime being now pretty well wafhed away, a fmall Collation waits upon him. He wonders much, and is refiefhed. That very Evening he is carried, gag'd and blinded, to a little Houfe near the Water-fide, where he is again locked up, but is much better treated than at the *Jew's* · Here he paffed a Part of the Night in no very comfortable Condition.

The Horror of his late Punifhment, and the Apprehenfion of fomething worfe that might enfue, fat troublefome upon his Mind. He has an eager longing after a Knowledge of Futurity— He wifhes any Weight were thrown in, to fink the Scale of Certainty. For to him, in his prefent Situation, fufpenfe, that neutral State, that neither one Thing nor another, was much worſe than the moſt poſitive Evil that could happen.

One Reflection ſtill remained to comfort him, the Purity of his Intention, and his filial Integrity which prompted him to bring over Proſelytes from all Religions to his ſpiritual Mother, the Church of *England*. This was the Staff on which his Virtue leaned. In this he found a Prop for all Afflictions Nay, he looked upon himſelf, in ſome ſort, to be a Martyr ; and was determined to perſevere.

In the midſt of theſe ſolemn Reflections, what was his Amazement, to ſee enter the Chamber, one of his Body Guards, with a Sabre and a Lanthorn ; who commanded our Miſſionary to riſe and follow him, without ſpeaking one Word The Doctor did ſo. - He led him through back Lanes and narrow Streets, to where a Coach ſtood, at the Extremity of the Town ; then, pointing to him to ſtep into it, he made his Bow and ſuddenly was gone.

The Doctor obeyed, and met in the Coach a gay young Chevalier, richly habited, who made a ſign to him to continue ſilent. The Coach roll'd away with Speed ; and, when the Morning appeared, he found himſelf four Leagues from the City of *Amſterdam*. His Fellow-Traveller had been upon the reſerve till now ; when, with the riſing Sun, he revealed himſelf, and with equal Beauty ſhone upon the World. It was indeed the charming *Deborah*, the Doctor's Patient and enlightened Proſelyte, that was her Name, the *Jew's* Daughter who had contrived this Method of Eſcape for her two-fold Phyſician. They embrace, rejoice—Oh ſuch a Change of Fortune ! They whirl on to the *Hague*, with Deſign to embark for *England*.

Deborah

Deborah had taken Care to fecure a large Sum, with Diamonds of great Value. They are arrived —took Lodgings —Our Chevalier lived with his lovely Convert, who walked in her Difguife (of a young Gentleman of Quality) during their Abode in this agreeable Place.

It was the Doctor's Lot (whofe Life muft be chequered) to meet, at a Vifit which he made to a Clergyman, his Friend, a renegado Friar, of the Order of St. *Dominic*, who, having fled from his Convent on meer religious Motives, came to *Holland*, to abjure the *Popifh*, and embrace the *Proteftant* Communion. The Minifter, to whom he addreffed himfelf, promifed to apply to the Government in his Favour. He told him, the Doctor was an earneft good *Proteftant* and an *Englifhman*; to whom he might with great Safety, unbofom himfelf. He advifed him to lodge in the fame Houfe with the Doctor, till his Affairs were fettled. The Doctor invited him heartily to his Hotel, whither the *Dutch* Parfon, the *French* Friar, and the *Ubiquitarian* Chevalier quickly repaired.

The Friar foon appeared to be a Gentleman of fine Tafte and Learning, together with an Addrefs and Politenefs far above the Sphere of St. *Dominic*

The Friar and the Doctor grew every Day more and more good Friends—they agree to fet out together for *England*. The Friar was far from being poor. A Fortnight paffed in this agreeable Situation. The handfome *Deborah* ftill making one of the Company, in Character of our Chevalier's Kinfman. Never did Dr. *Taylor* pafs a more agreeable Interval.

The Friar, by this Time, had caft his Coat, and appeared in a brilliant Habit, which beft became him. He fung, he danced, was witty, told a Story admirably.   He often amufed himfelf with the Doctor's Coufin at a Game at Chefs. He did every Thing with a Grace and Manner which fpoke the higheft Breeding, without the leaft Pedantry.   He faid, It was his Difguife ; for he expected every Moment to be purfued from *France*, as he was a Perfon of Family, and had renounced his Religion.

In fhort, *Deborah* and he exchanged one Confidence for another ; and, by unbottoning a little, *Deborah* made no Scruple, at laft, of letting the Friar into her whole Story.   She begged his Advice and Affiftance, which he gave, and promifed her with great Gladnefs.   They fat whole Afternoons together ; when the Friar, to divert his Anxiety, would make her fome Tenders of Gallantry, not with any ferious Intention to be fure ;, but rather as an Exercife of his Faculties, and to diffipate the Lady's Chagrine But the next Chapter fhall inform you, how far his Philofophy was a Match for his Love, and what followed in Confequence thereof

C H A P. IV.

The Reader has now the Clue in his Hand , and,
without conjuring, may guefs at what follows in
this Chapter.   But he fhall know the Particulars.

THIS friendly Traffick went on, it feems, with warm Succefs , and refined itfelf into fomething more feraphic than meer Good-will, or what the unfeeling Part of Mankind call Friendfhip.   There was Sentiment it's true, in this Exchange of Kindnefs : But meer Sentiment is too cold a Commerce.   The Pathetic and the Heart

must

muſt be infuſed. The Friar himſelf explained it all, and put his Leſſon into Practice with great Energy of Soul ; nor was *Deborah* a whit behind in her Proportion ; as the Chevalier himſelf, with ſome Emotion, was ſoon convinced of, at his Return from viſiting his Friend the Clergyman ; who charged him with ſome important Meſſage to the Friar. For he was now purſued from *France*

I ſay the Chevalier, coming to his Lodgings in great Haſte, and ſtepping up Stairs to acquaint his Friend with what he heard, he there ſurprized *Deborah* and Father *Dominic* much in the ſame Attitude and Employment that Mrs. *Brady* had ſeen him and his Bride *Jenny*. The Doctor, no ſtrict Votary to Virtue himſelf, felt upon this Occaſion a kind of Reſentment, that aroſe rather from Intereſt than Principle.

Deborah had got ſome Hold on his Affections and Gratitude, and the Friar on his Friendſhip ; both which he found a little troubleſome to part with at one Pluck. He was tempted to break open the Door for that was locked, and reek his Vengeance at a Blow. But Prudence this once put herſelf between him and his Paſſion. He fretted, pauſed, conſidered, and ſo went down Stairs again with full Reſolution to tell the Parſon what a hopeful Pair of Proſelytes they had got in hand.

He no ſooner turned the Corner of the Street, than he met with one *O' Farrel*, an *Iriſh* Gentleman then in the *French* Service, whom he knew formerly in *London* ; where he healed up ſeveral Scars received by the Captain in the Wars of *Venus*.

O' Farrel embraced him with great Show of Friendſhip ; and told him, There was a Countryman of his, an Eccleſiaſtic of great Diſtinction,

with

with whom he would make him acquainted; and begged the Honour of his Company to dine with them that Day, if not engaged.

The Doctor made no Scruple to comply in hopes it might diffipate the Chagrin his late Difcovery had occafioned.—So together they went to a Tavern, where they dined very chearfully, and drank a Bottle of the beft.

O' Farrel, as he grew warm told the Doctor, he would acquaint him, in Confidence of his Friendfhip, with an Affair of fome Moment; not doubting in the leaft of his Advice and Affiftance.

To which *Taylor* anfwered, fay on, and never doubt me.

Then fays *O' Farrel*, I am to tell you, Sir, that my Friend the Clergyman and I are come into *Holland*, in purfuit of a Gentleman, a Brother of his Order, who has unhappily eloped from his Convent. But that is not all, added the Captain; he has carried off with him, a Sum of Money, and Jewels, of great Value, the Property of a young Lady his own Kinfwoman: For indeed he is come of a very good Family. And this ugly Slip, fays he, will be a great Difgrace to his Family, and his Order befide. I would give a good deal to hear of him.

The Doctor inftantly fmoked the Affair; and afked them fome leading Queftions. Every Thing tally'd exactly. They drew the Friar's Picture to a Hair.

And now our Chevalier's Mind began to work. He held a Council within. There Jealoufy and Refentment opened the Caufe in Favour of *O' Farrel* and his Friend. They pleaded warmly. But, on the other Hand, Honour, Friendfhip and Gratitude would needs be heard too. They made

some

come Impreſſion; and the Ballance now was al-
moſt equal.

When *O' Fairel*'s Friend, perceiving the Doctor's Suſpenſe, told him with great Franknefs,
that he judged him to be more a Gentleman and
a good Chriſtian, than to refuſe his Aid in ſo
laudable an Affair, as bringing a foul Criminal
to Juſtice: So faying, he pulled from his Finger
a Ring of ſome Value, which he begged the
Doctor would accept of; nay he put it on himfelf.

This was too much—this turned the Scale.
And Father *Dominic* and Miſs *Deby* were both
miſſing the next Day. The Thing made a Noiſe.
—The Parſon, enquiring at the Lodging, was
told, That the Chevalier went out in the Morning, but did not return as uſual to Dinner; but
ſent a Coach in the Evening with an Invitation
to the two Gentlemen to ſup with him at a
Tavern.

The Parſon applied to the Government, who
offered a Sum for bringing back the Friar; and
ordered all the *Roman Catholic* Clergy in that
Diſtrict to be put into cloſe Confinement, till Father
Dominic was forth-coming.

The Doctor took to his Heels, well knowing
that the Conſequence would be fatal to him.
He took Shipping with a good round Sum in his
Pocket, and landed in *England*, with a Mixture
in his Mind of Triumph and Remorſe.

CHAP. V.

Here the Scene is changed; and the Subject, it is
hoped, will not be less entertaining in the Sequel.

HE appears grand, and made some Progress
in his Fame for giving Light, with the other
professional Feats: For he practised yet as a Physician and Surgeon.

In general he became more and more extravagant He grew giddy with Success, and overshot
all Bounds.—He is again brought low in Fortune.
When meeting with a Mountebank in the West
of *England*, he agreed to join him with all the Stock
of Knowledge, Effrontery, Dexterity, Elocution
and Address, which he had gathered up on the Con-
and elsewhere.

No General was ever better qualified to take the
Field, than was our Doctor to mount the Stage
itinerant.

Bills were printed for the first Time, and handed
about, those constant Postillions of his Fame, his
Forerunners ever after, to signify that a regular
bred Artist, out of meer Humanity, had for the
first Time, condescended to appear on high, for
the public Good. He had prepared an elaborate
and eloquent Oration, which Fate and a rainy
Day hindered him from delivering. But as the
Original is in our Hands, we will give it to the
Reader in the Words that follow :

The Mountebank's Speech.

THE Nature of Good, my worthy Countrymen, is to communicate itself. Good is a
communicative Thing. Good is not selfish, or
solitary. Good is no Good, except it is diffused.
Good

Good, like a Dunghill, is good for nothing, till it is spread about; and for the Matter of that, no more is a heap of Gold itself

This Remark the Banker and the Husbandman will judge a good one. The Miser may perhaps put in his Exception; but my Lord *Bacon* and the Gold Finder will both tell him, that he lies. And, what is Gold; or even Dung itself, a much more useful Commodity? I say, what is either of them, or both of them, when they are compared to the Manure of the Mind? when they are compared to Knowledge, to saving Knowledge, such saving Knowledge is the greatest Good of Mortals? Gold and Dung, are Creatures of the Earth; Knowledge is the Child of Heaven. A Thief may steal the Gold, and Farmers carry off the Dung; but, Gentlemen, no Thief, but Death, can rob you of your Knowledge

Knowledge is your own; a Treasure within you, which can never be made less by sharing it with a Friend.

That's another Point, in which it flogs your Gold. He that has Knowledge, and will not communicate, is the worst of Misers. Knowledge is the Food of the Mind, and the Medicine of the Body.

But, must a Man of Skill, therefore, keep a Preacher's or a Chemist's Shop, sit still and expect his Neighbours to come in with their Money and purchase by the Pound? No, Gentlemen, a Man of benevolent Parts, who loves the World, must go abroad, must travel with his Ware, not like a fat old, rich Brazier, who sits behind his Counter exchanging his Dross for real Gold No, Sirs, but like an honest Tinker, who trots about from Place to Place, who rings his Brass, and brings the Bees together. He can mend the

House-

Houfewife's leaky Kettle in her own Sight and Hearing; and her Hufband too may fee him do it. —

Parifh Parfons are lazy Fellows. Once a Week, indeed, they open Houfe, ferve up the fame old-fafhoned Mefs, and all the Country far and near, muft come to hear them forfooth.

The trading Juftice is another fedentary Rogue, who leans upon his Elbow in his Office, and makes the Bible do the Devil's Work.

The Apothecary, Gentlemen, is a Knave, who keeps his Poifon in a Heap, and makes it ftill more rank, by lying long together.

The Mountebank, my Friends, or travelling Leech, he gives his Medicines Air; they travel with himfelf, for Health; and what they gain by going about they give.

The Mountebank's the Man of faving Knowledge. He'll keep no Shop neither, like the Preacher, Chemift, Brazier, Parfon, trading Juftice, or Apothecary, thefe local, lazy Weeds, that fatten and rot upon the Ground they cumber.

The Mountebank is like the Tinker in his Trudge, the Judge upon his Circuit, the Bifhop in his Vifitation, the Doctor in his Country Call, and *Whitefield* in his Province. —

The Mountebank, or Travelling-Doctor is like the Sun, the Patron of his Art, he fhines out far and near; he blazes as he travels.

Publick Spirit, among the *Greeks* and *Romans*, was reckoned the higheft Virtue. The Perfon who poffefled that noble Quality, was called a Patriot.

A Man might be a Patriot, in thofe Days, without ftirring much abroad. If he travelled to the Town-Houfe, from fome neighbouring Street, and there got up upon what they called, a Roftium, or fomething made of old Ships Rudders, and

talked

talked an Hour or fo, about Corruption, Liberty
and the King of *Parthia*, his Work was done at
once; the Alderman was dubb'd a Patriot, and all
the Neighbours worfhipped him.   How cheap was
Honour purchafed in thofe Days? In latter Ages
the Thing was better underftood, when the prince-
ly Fafhion of Knight-Errantry firft prevailed in the
World.   Then did the true publick Spirit kindle
up the Souls of Heroes, pious Sons of Hardy-
hood and Honour, to fally forth in Defence of Innocence oppreffed and injured Virtue, forfaking all
for Honour's fake, and wedding as it were their
Virtue to the publick Good, not like our modern
Militia, who grumble at lofing fight of their own
Dunghills.   Thefe Gentlemen bid farewel to all
domeftic Allurements, Forefts, Heaths, inchanted
Caves, and Caftles, Giants, Rogues and Robbers,
and all the Inftruments and Powers of Darknefs;
with thefe they waged inceffant War, in fpight
of Hunger and Cold, in fpite of Toil and Danger,
in fpite of broken heads and broken Ribs, they
ftill rode on triumphant, they were Honour's true
Apoftles; nay they fuffered Martyrdom in fighting
for that Goddefs.   The renowned *Quixote* will
inform you more.

What think you then, Gentlemen, of us who
ftand before you in this exalted Light? What think
you, Sirs, of me who trampling on all Temptations,
to fit ftill fpurning at Wealth and Grandeur,
Diftinction and Applaufe, who, I fay, in fpite of
all this, have made myfelf a Footftool of thefe very Motives, in Order to raife me up to this exalted Station?

I am now the talleft Man among five Thoufand.
I look down upon you all, but it is with the Eyes
of Pity and compaffion for your many Ailments
and Infirmities.   My healing Dews fhall foon de-
fcend upon you.   My Medicine, like the Manna

in the Wilderness, shall fall in Showers around you, and restore your Peace.

I am the Man of Knowledge, mentioned as above, who scorned to sit at Home, and deal it out in Scruples.

I am the communicative Man, who gives it to his Friends in Handfuls. My Manna I spread about, my Gold I circulate; my Virtue shall revive you, my Knowledge shall preserve you.

I am your Champion in the Cause of Health. I trample down the Dragon called Disease. I pull out his Sting and send him soon a packing.

No Hospital shall stand hereafter, with Charity on the Face, and Knavery in the Heart. No Lazar-House, these Sores of Honesty, shall hence infect the Land, and rob the Purses of the Public to bolster up the Lazy, and the Ignorant. No, Gentlemen, these Citadels of Fraud shall soon be scattered.

Behold the Bullet that shall demolish them. This Pill, this mighty Pill, when shot from the Artillery of my Knowledge, shall lay them all in Rubbish.

This Bullet shall destroy that Python the Apothecary, and Health and Honesty shall sing afresh through the Land.

This Pill shall counteract *Pandora's* Box, and drive away all physical and moral Evils; that is, Gentlemen, all Disease and Doctors. No *Rock* shall then remain; no *French* Distemper, no Pill, or Drop, excepting mine, shall soon be heard of; no glittering Equipage to dazzle vulgar Eyes; no boisterous Eloquence to stun their Ears. This little Pill shall do the Work in Silence. It is a World of healing Virtue, a Globe of salutary Good; nor need you dig into its Bowels for the precious Balm, it is all but one continued Virtue unmixed, one pure Elixir unalloyed, the Surface

and

and the Center are the fame; it is a Univerfe of Good, the true Catholicon of Man.

Let no Horrors henceforth hang upon the fierce Embrace of rapid Lovers, or damp their extatic Joy with Apprehenfions of the foul Difeafe. This little *Noftrum* is your Sword and Buckler; this fhall beat down every *French* Antagonift: This is your *Palladium*. This precious Shield was dropped from Heaven. This Heal-ftone of the friendly Atmofphere.

James's Powders are not more potent in their Province, that Foe to Fevers.

But mark me, Sirs, this little Pill is like the King of *Pruffia*. It is a Match for many. It refemb-leth, in its Power the Rod of *Aaron*. It fwallow-eth up all other Medicines and Difeafes too. It is in that refpect the Gulph of all human Care.

Confider then, my Countrymen, had I fat ftill at Home, and kept this mighty Secret to myfelf, what would become of the bulk of mankind? One City, or Town, perhaps had reaped the Benefit of this amazing Medicine, a Medicine of more Uti-lity to Mankind than all the Longitudes, and per-petual Motions in the World. I fay, this inefti-mable Pill might then have rendered immortal a Parifh or two. Perhaps that is the narrow Cir-cle of my own particular Cuftomers, whilft all the Sons and Daughters of *Adam* befides, were left a Prey to Apothecaries, Quacks, Difeafe and Death. Ah! what a dreadful Confequence muft have followed fuch a local Caft of Mind in me: But, Thanks to Heaven, my Dwelling is the Univerfe.

The World's a wife Man's Home What a Wretch were I, if the Love of Money, or the Love of Eafe had fixed me, like a Pump or Pil-lory, to one fordid Spot! No, Gentlemen, a ftrong Philanthropy had feized my Heart. I look-

ed

ed abroad with Pity on my Kind——my Bowels yearned on the human Race. In ſhort I ſold off all, joined with Dr. *Green*; and here I ſtand before you, in the Prime of Youth and Vigour, with all my Faculties of Mind and Body in their utmoſt Prime, at their vertic Point of high Perfection: Every Thought and Sentiment, every Joint and Member I conſecrate to publick Uſe. Myſelf, and all I have, I dedicate to you.

Alcides, in his Time, was ſuch a Man as I am. His Knowledge, Courage, Virtue, Strength, his Club, and all were offered to his Country's Service. He travelled far and near, and made the World the better for him.

Æſculapius himſelf, the Father of the Faculty, was a Sort of Mountebank: He went about, its true, on Foot; nor is it fully clear, that he mounted any Stage; Tradition there is ſomething doubtful. But he went about, he culled his Simples, and he milked his Goats, adminiſtring as he went from Town to Town; nor did his Dog remain behind him. He dreamt not of a gilded Chariot, or a ſhining Fee, nor was he warmed by a chymic Fire. He never heard a mortar ring in all his Life. A Clyſter-Pipe was then as little known as Printing.

It is a Doubt among the learned, if ever *Æſculapius* felt a Pulſe, or not. In this they all agree, he did not cure a Clap. *Æſculapius*, Sirs, was nothing if compared to me. And let me ſpeak it out, the breathing tribe of all his preſent Sons this little Pill ſhall ſuperſede. The Faculty ſhall fall, and Funerals ſhall be ſcarce. The Sexton, in Deſpair, ſhall throw his Spade aſide, and dance about with Bear and Fiddle. The Parſon ſhall feed on Chriſtenings and Weddings. The Wedding Muſic and the Morning Drum ſhall oft be heard; but ſeldom, ſeldom ſhall the Paſſing-Bell

athwart

athwart the evening Concert toll, and mix Morta-
lity with Mufic. The Undertakers then fhall all
turn Dancing-Mafters ; and Doctors play upon
the Pipe and Tabor. Their moral Caterers, the
juft Apothecaries, fhall fling their Gallipots upon
the Dunghill, fell Salloop at Corners, to Shoe-blacks,
and to *Strand*-Walkers; or open Cooks-Shops in
Porrage-Ifland, Vinegar-Yard, and *Long-Ditch,
Weftminfter* ; inftead of Pills and Drugs, to drefs
up Beef and Cabbage for Carmen, and for Porters.

Oh ! what a Falling-off is this ! How many
Volumes then fhall greedy *Vulcan* fwallow !
What *Vaticans* of medical Report fhall then be
filent ? How poor Hypothefis fhall bleed ? I fpeak
to you the Attorneys of the Faculty, you Clyfter-
giving Tribe : I fee you grin with murky, lowring
Looks, with meagre, cloudy, gallows Faces ; your
Chariots fhall come down ; you'll foot about again
in fultry Weather, and turn the Tallow in your
Faces to red. You'll give good Pennyworths in
the *Strand* again ; that's the Market for Salloop.

How Guefs-work now fhall go to wreck ! How
hoar Credulity fhall drop her Looking-Glafs and
Spectacles, and grope about for fomething certain !
How vain-Authority fhall then look blank ! when
Learning urg'd by Truth, fhall open but her
mufty Roll, and fling the ftale commiffion, by fome
few Exceptions, in this general Wreck. — Merit,
immortal Merit, makes Sages, that are Proof to
Fire ; whofe Books are incumbuftible, and only
with the World fhall burn.

I fee the Hand of pure, impartial Criticifm cull
them from among the Heaps of Tinder, juft
catching at the Flame, and place them high upon
the fame Shelf with *Bacon, Lock* and *Tully*, with
Addifon and *Plato* ; thefe Authors are but few
who efcape the fiery Trial, the *English* ones I
mean ; and Foreigners, I fear, are fewer ftill ; the
Names.

Names I think are, *Sydenham*, *Freind*, *Wellwood*,
Garth and *Mead*, these of former Times. The
present Sons of Practice are equal in their Claim,
and shall live as long as they did; that is till they
die.   But then their Works shall stay behind them,
and look as fresh as theirs at Doom's-Day.

Let me see, in this Hurry, none but First-rates
will be visible. O, aye, there's *Hulse* and *Heber-
den*, sagacious learned *Nugent*, and my lively
Name's sake *Taylor*, a polished little Gem; these
may go on out of meer Decency, while they
chuse; but the Business drops with them. They
must not propagate.

What a wonderful working Pill is this!—The
Doctors and the Water-men shall be useless soon
alike; the one, when the new Bridge is built; and
the other, when I have got my Patent. Why, I
shall drive these Fellows out of Fashion, as the
Musquet did the Bow and Arrow. My Bullet
here, this little Pill, is worth a thousand Archers.
These Sons of *Phœbus* shall shoot their Shafts no
more against the Moon, and wound the Patient's
Pocket

My honest Battery is levelled at the whole Alli-
ance of all human Maladies   Down they go, at one
invincible Broadside. What need so many Ways
to dispatch poor *Towser*, since one will do?

Brevity in Business, Gentlemen, is the Life of
Trade. What Statues, Sirs, what Columns shall
be reared to me! But not at *Spaw*, at *Bristol*,
or at *Bath*, nor yet at *Leyden*. My Trophies
shall ascend in Cities full of Luxury, where riots
Joy, where *Venus*, *Bacchus*, and the Muses make
their lov'd Abode, where Pleasure reigns unsoil'd
by Care, and Mirth and Fancy sweep the gay
Horizon; that is, they'll like me better at St.
James's End of the Town, than at *White Chapel*;
at *Arthur*'s, better than at *Lloyd*'s: Though now
of

of late, as Things have taken a Turn, 'tis hard to tell the Courtier from the Pedlar, the *Exchange*, forsooth is like the Drawing-Room, though a little aukward in the Copy, as once the Ass would imitate the Spaniel When Tradesmen's Wigs are hung with empty Bags to them, I tremble for their Heads and Pockets.

Should old Sir *Thomas Gresham* animate his *Gothic* Statue, and look from thence upon his metamorphos'd Acre, he would bless himself, and think, that all *America* had sent her mimic Tribes to practise Counting-House Conges, where *Walsingham* and *Burleigh* used to meet; for they would mix with Merchants. Merchants are the Pillars of the State, robust and plain, the *Tuscan* or the *Doric* if you will. Their Office is to stand abroad, to bear up the Weight of all the incumbent Palace. The soft exuberant, *Corinthian*; or the Harlot decked, wanton, proud *Composite*, should rank for idle Ornaments within, and not support. Tear off ye Sons of Traffic, these gaudy good-for-nothing Trifles, give them back again to *French* Lacquies, to Fencing-Masters, to fifth-rate Players, to Opera Things. Let not a Citizen be seen to wear them. Let the Citizen rejoice in this. This is his Shirt of Mail, his Shield and Buckler in the Walks of *Covent* Garden, his *Viaticum*, his Antidote, his Safeguard in that Episode of Peril.

This Pill, this single Pill is worth a Plumb on the other Side of *Temple-Bar*. The aldermanic, sober Merchant, with this Preventive in his Pocket, may visit the Exchange in *Bow-Street* without an oil'd Surtout; He may traffic in all Weathers, and take *Jenny Douglas* at her Word; nor need he dread a Quarantine at Home. No Family fasts on that Account. Inestimable Pill! It is Love's Insurance-Ticket, given out at *Cupid*'s own
Fire-

Fire-Office. It is an Amulet. It is a Miracle of Military Virtue, at perpetual War with every Thing that gives Disease.

How the Rheumatism, Gravel, Gout and Cholick, with all the veteran Phalanx, and the light-armed Troops, the whole chronic Camp, with every black Battalion, shall lay their dreaded Banners at my Feet, and beg for soft Conditions; but Hah! this envious Rain seems to take their Part, and is indeed their old Confederate. But let it deluge on; not all the Elements, with Luxury combined, shall stand against this Pill; nay, not all the Faculty to aid them, and their destructive Equipage to boot.

But the Rain, I see, will scatter us. It may prevent my Eloquence, but not my Art. You need not fear a Cold; here is your Riding-Coat and Boots. But still it comes down faster. The Prince of air has Notice of my Pill, and takes this Method to prevent its Virtue; it is like his antient Pranks. Some Conjurer has set him on. Aye, it thunders too — it is Time to go — I have got no Shield against Lightning. That Laurel is to spring. Hah, hah, that flash came near my Whiskers. We must break up. There's a Rattle for you! How it rumbles round the hollow Cieling! Another big Broad-side — down I come — 'tis Time to house — it spoiled my fine Oration but my Pill is dry.

Farewel, my honest Gentlemen and worthy Friends. Remember what I have said — This Storm has broke in upon me — We'll meet again on *Saturday.*

CHAP.

CHAP. VI.

Here our Incidents are shifting Time and Place continually; which will afford a chequered Tale indeed. But the Reader will not take our Word, I hope.

A Gentleman of the Faculty, in that Neighbourhood, had the Curiosity to find who this regular Adventurer could be He meets the Doctor, and discovers in him so much real Merit, that he persuaded him of all Things to check the Ambition which spurred him to ascend the Stage. And finding Necessity was as much in Fault as the Doctor's Inclination, he generously lent him a Sum of Money to set up once more with, and rescued, by that Means, our incomparable Artist from the Brand of a common Mountebank.

Here he stood **his ground** about sixteen Months, as Physician, Apothecary and Surgeon. But meeting with a Farmer's Daughter at a neighbouring Village, whom Mr. *Chefelden* had restored to Sight, it had the same Effect upon him that the Statue of *Alexander* at *Rhodes* had upon *Julius Cæsar*; his Soul distended at the Sight — he felt the God within him — he kindles with the Love of Glory, sells off his Shop and Surgeon's Implements, that vulgar Apparatus ; he pays the Gentleman the Sum he lent him, and with the few remaining Pieces sets of in a Coach and four, very early in the Morning.

He commences Oculist solely, renouncing all Commerce with any mechanic and degrading Professions, as he called them. He writes a Treatise upon Cataracts, which was soon republished, and dedicated, in a very pompous Stile, to the late Queen.

He

He travels Northward like the Sun, giving Light and Joy.

In his Journey he performed several amazing Cures, at *New-Castle* and elsewhere.

He passes the *Tweed*, followed and preceded with Fame and Applause. He enters *Scotland*, ascends the Capital, gets Money in Handfuls, lectures in Public, makes a fine Display of his Eloquence and Diamond Ring. He pays his Addresses to a young Lady, who had a handsome Fortune, for that Country, and made Advances towards Matrimony.

Her Uncle, a Kirk Minister, and a wary Man, in whose hands her Fortune lay, had a sharp Lookout. He writes to a Friend at the *Bath*, who knew the Doctor's Story; is immediately answered, that the Doctor has been married many Years; that his Wife is living, together with a handsome Boy a Son of his. All this, says the *Bath* Friend, I know to be true. The Son is now at School in *Kensington*, and his Wife lodges with my Relation at *Chelsea*.

The young Lady, it seems, had made a private Treaty with the Doctor, and they were just upon the Brink of signing and sealing, when her Uncle shews her the Letter; and sending for the Doctor, he did him the same Favour, which so thunder-struck our detected Chevalier, that he confessed the whole Matter, said he meant nothing more than a little Amusement, begged ten thousand Pardons, and rushed into the Street.

Edinburgh is now too hot for him. He scampers off that Night, and takes shipping for *Ireland*. He lands at *Dublin* — is well received — gives a *Syllabus* — lectures in Public *gratis*.

Here he is followed by People of Fashion who invite and caress him; for bating a little of the Knight-Errant, which from our Doctor is inseparable,

rable, there was something whimsical and not dis-
agreeable mixed with his Manner.   His Style,
though it sometimes bordered upon the Burlesque,
yet his Deportment was so rapid and shining, one
had not Time to reckon the Ridiculous, it was
carried off in the Vortex of his Elocution, which
made an Impression, tho' singular indeed, yet not
unpleasing; it puts one in Mind of the Poem,
called, *The Splendid Shilling*.

Here he met with Money, Politeness and Hospitality.   But his left-handed Genius could not stand
by and see him succeed so well, without dashing
his Cup with a little Bitter.

He meets with an unfortunate Rub.   A young
Gentleman, under his Care, had by his own Mis-
conduct, in getting Cold, and an Inflammation in
Consequence, lost the Use of one of his Eyes.
He was a member of the University, and a Person
of Family.

He with his Friends affected to hope that his
Case was not desperate.

They invite Dr. *Taylor* to meet, at the Gentleman's Chambers, two learned Men of the Faculty,
in Order to consult what more could be done
for the Patient.   The Doctor attends, dressed in
a Suit of rich Velvet.   He is received at the Stair-
foot by a Person in a black Gown, who hands him
up into a large Room, hung with Cloth of the
same Colour, where one Funereal Lamp afford-
ed a Kind of Darkness visible, which quickly
served to discover the Sights of Woe; for now the
Gentleman had left him, and was soon succeeded by
a Dozen frightful Spectres in the Shape of Furies, who made a dreadful Yelling in his Ears,
one of them continually crying out, Oh, *Taylor,
Taylor,* give me back my Eyes   They spit Fire at
him, and play a thousand horrid Pranks.   The
Doctor, thinks himself in *Lucifer*'s Salloon, when

presently

prefently his Body is inverted, his Heels are drawn up to the Cieling, and his Head now pointing to the Center, when lo! a large Cedar Refervoir is thrown open very near his Nofe, and ftirred up from the Bottom by a Dozen reeking red hot Pokers. Reader, imagine what favoury Exhalations muft afcend, it ftupified his earthly Senfes.

Overcome by fuch exceffive Odour he hung intranced All Marks of Life were fled, feeing, hearing, nay fmelling are to him but Things indifferent; fo totally abftracted was his Senforium.

The Fiends relent, they let him down at laft He lies motionlefs a-while, with ftaring Eye-Balls and with lolling Tongue.

They let in Air. He returns unwilling to the hated Light. He breathes, he groans, he fnorts, he cries out, Murder. The Watchmen, to whom he is now configned, take Poffeffion of the fumigated Doctor. They bear him to the Round-Houfe.

One Comfort ftill among his Sufferings ftuck by him; his Money, Watch, his Diamond Crofs and Ring were all fafe. They were, indeed, a little tarnifhed, and fuffered, like himfelf, a fad Eclipfe. He took Snuff immeafurably, and caft about his aromatic Effence. Nothing could fweeten his polluted Fancy. The Cedar Cheft and fiery Pokers were ftill reeking in his Brain. He wifhed for the *Dutchman*'s Ciftern and all its rufhing Streams. His Imagination ftunk. Not all *Arabia* could perfume that Box. The Watchmen, nay the Gold-finders now ftand aloof; no human Nofe could bear it. Nor is even this the worft Indignity: *A bad Name,* as *Solomon* fays, *is worfe than forty Fumigations;* there, alas! it ftung him. No Friend, no Medicine but Defpair

O *Taylor!* yes, there is a Medicine, there is a Friend at Hand; *Dick Eagle* is at Hand, with broken

ken

ken Fore-head and with blackened Eye; for he has boxed with *Paddy Cryfty* the College Scull, who came athwart him in the Paths of Pimping; *Dick Eagle* is at Hand—How Friends will meet! They ftand, they ftare, they ftink together; for *Dicky's* Galligafkins were difhonoured. Affliction makes Men Friends. They gaze again with Grief and Wonder.

In *Dicky's* Face the Rafcal was predominant amidft his Woes, and claimed a Kind of *Tyburn* Pity. He hung his ignominious Head depreffed by Guilt, and all his Looks proclaimed the Scoundrel— The Doctor burft out firft, for he had lefs of Blame: O fatal Meeting! the laft was in a Round-Houfe: How efcaped you *Newgate*—the Furrier's Wife from *Kingfton*, Sir *Francis*, *Sodom*, fetting your own Houfe, Baron *Pengelly?* but I forgive you all— the Storm has caft us on a Rock. O, *Richard Eagle*, let us now be Friends, and Friends they were, a Coach is called, the Watch are paid, but *David Dove* will find out all To-morrow.

At *Dicky's* Houfe they ftop, it was an hofpitable Door; he comforted his Friend; the Doctor in Return explores his battered Orb, and pours in lenient Medicines. It was a Houfe of fair Reception, where twenty Beds at leaft were ftanding. Such was *Dicky's* Tafte of Hofpitality, magnificent and like the Manner of the Eaft. Yea there were in it Damfels of a pleafing Hue, fuch as *Dicky's* wealthy Friends would oft vouchfafe to vifit. In that it differed from the Mode of *Perfia*; for here the Sexes met at large and trafficked. Yea it was called Love's Exchange. The good Town were fometimes fmuggled; for Wives and Daughters were often afked for at *Dicky's* Door, here the Doctor lay; and *Dicky's* Eye grew better.

CHAP.

CHAP. VII.

In this Section we are resolved to let the Story speak for itself, and shall not give a Bill of Fare at all.

BUT Fame, that tatling Pest, was now abroad. The Fumigation rose like Incense at the Altar of Detraction, grateful to the Nostril of the sneering Faculty, but t David and *Jenny Dove*, eternal Triumph. His C was gratified. To work he went, with Malice oiling over; and now a Print appears, where, dr ul to behold, the fatal Process is at large displayed. There hung the Doctor with his Heels aloft. The Pokers here and Closestool were at work, the putrid Essence in a Cloud ascends, the Furies stir up all its Malice, the dismal Lamp glimmereth sadly over the Scene, and underneath, alas! were Verses—What Cellar, what Stall, what Garret, or what Bogg-house hath not seen the Picture?

Philosophy herself was here abashed, and even Fortitude turned pale No Comfort but the Cordials of his Friend, I mean of Mr. *Richard Eagle*, now was left him.

He sung, he danced, he played, and now and then, by way of soft Relief, he brought his Friend a Whore; the Face he brought was always new, for *Dicky*'s Flock could then afford it.

Thus shut in a whole Fortnight from the Sight of Men was the Doctor. But *Dicky*'s Eye grew better; he beats about, he dines with *Humphry Gibbet*, Esq. There he saw the fair *Linnetta*, her Feature was alluring, her Eye was waggish, and her Voice was Rapture.

Dicky's Soul had fastened on her, and General *Pay-well* has a Mind to see her. The Trains are set; the Snair is fixed; *Linnetta* now improves her

Notes

Notes at *Lazars-hill,* and *Humphry Gibbet* is almost run mad. Revenge has Eyes like *Argos.*

Linnetta's Cage is now no more a Secret, and *Humphry Gibbet* is resolved to have her back. He comes at Midnight with a Band of Ruffians, Sons of *Belial*; Swords, Pistols, and other Instruments of Mischief were not wanting; these were chosen Men of *Humphry's* own Battalion.

To *Dicky's* Door they come, and soon find Entrance, the Servant is corrupted.

With Torches, and with Vizors, on they marched up the Stairs. They stand, they listen, for now a gentle Earthquake seems to shake the Floor, the Factory was all at work, a Dozen Beds at least were jogging. Zounds, what s here, says *Humphry Gibbet,* the Forge of Propagation? Sure all the Sledges are at work, the *Cyclops* at their Anvils O damn me, Sparks, I'll spoil your Sport; where is this Prince of Pimps? where is this Villain *Eagle?*

Not here, not here, cries out a frighted Parson in his Pannic, and leaps upon the Floor—nor here, a ghastly aged Lawyer on his Knees cries out, take Pity on my Years; I did not shake the Rafters. Black Rock Water! nothing now will do. Here, here's the Villain *Eagle,* and here's *Linnetta* too, and here is Doctor *Fumble,* and Major *Trailpike* with his shaking Head, and *Circumsloiterous* with his algebraic Mien. Was ever such a Nest of Sinners? Drag out that Rascal *Eagle.* Oh, here he is, an't please your Honour. I have him; call the Porters; get the Blanket ready; where's the Frying Pan, the Horn and Fiddles?

Lo! now, Reader, beginneth the Apotheosis of Mr. *Richard Eagle.* A frosty Night it was; the northern Bear bit very close. Lo! *Richard,* in his Shirt is led, or rather carried into the outward Court, beneath the spangling Vault of Heaven, where every angry Star was witness.

Four big-bon̄ed, ſturdy, ugly Villains, with Vi-zers on, ſtood facing one another at right Angles, in an oblong Form, holding each the Corner of a Blanket.   With both their Hands they held it, and often ſhook and ſtretched the elaſtic Mantle.

Dick beheld his Fate and ten-fold trembled What Wonder, ſince Froſt, and Fear, and Shame, and Rage, and Spight, were warring now within, with-out, and round about him.

The Doctor could not help him, and *Humphry Gibbet* is inexorable—Toſs in the Scoundrel, toſs in this Pimp and Poet; keep Time, my Boys; ſtrike upon the Pan and Fiddle; let the Horn have Wind. Up he goes, he ſprings off finely; keep Time, the Muſic and the Blanket—that Stroke was well—he pukes—he ſprings again, at either End he guſhes; ſend him to the ſublime, and knock his Head againſt the Stars—What an Anticlimax !—how far he ſquirts it ! that Bounce for Lady *Linnetta*, that for Mrs. *Lindſey* O the lofty Pimp Pindaric *Dicky* ! how he ſoars all this while !

The Doctor at the Window ſaw with Sorrow, but could not help his Friend.   The Fumigation came a-freſh in his Mind But *Dicky*'s next Aſcent happening to be near the Wall, the Doctor, ſtretching out too far to catch him, fell at once up-on the Blanket in a cloſe Embrace with *Dick*.

They broke their Paſſage through it on the Ground; on the Ground they lay; they wallowed in the Filth, for *Dick* had vented much.

The Doctor now is bruiſed.   In *Dick* no Sign of Life remains, but his Manhood ſtill is viſible.   A-midſt theſe Shocks of Fortune, which added Firm-neſs, and with inborn Pride it looks aloft, and glo-ries in its Sufferings—*Humphry Gibbet* ſaw and won-dered.

The Muſic now is ſilent, and Mr. *Richard Eagle*, by *Humphry Gibbet*'s Order is wrapped up in
the

the broken Blanket and carried to his Bed, where the Doctor administred to him, and brought him by Degrees to his Senses.

Mean while *Linnetta* is carried off in Triumph by *Humphry Gibbet*, but not without Companions. Each Hero had his Nymph, which thinned not a little this Family of Love ; the Parson, Lawyer, and the rest, were glad to scamper off with whole Bones.

The Morning came at last, but no joyful Morn to *Dicky*. The Remembrance of what he felt; for he remembered Part was painful to him. He told his Friend, that, after a Bounce or two, he was like the Thieves at *Tyburn*, who lose all Sense at the first Swing; for so one half-hung *Smith* had told him; for he knew not of Puking, or what else he did ——

O Doctor, Doctor, give me but Revenge. My Girls all vanished ! *Linnetta* too ! Oh fatal Trade of Pimping ! What Bastinados are thy Due? but Virtue must endure.

Thus complained the afflicted Mr. *Richard Eagle*; for Shame for once had struck him. He durst not stir abroad. The Mob had got him in the Wind.

The Doctor grew more bold, he sallied forth, his Friends were glad to see him ; they resented his Abuse, and compelled the College Sparks to make Atonement in Public, and to beg the Doctor's Pardon. He mounts again the Rostrum, performs surprizing Cures, gets Money in Abundance, visits *Dick Eagle*, drags him from his Hole.

Dick appears, but, like the Bat, by Glimpses in the Evening A Blanket is his Bane. He trembles when he sees one.

The Doctor had now increased his Reputation and his Purse considerably. He takes a Trip to *Cork*, the second City of the Kingdom.

On

On the Road he meets with his evil Genius *Dove*, who had nailed, on the outside of his Chaise, the Prints of the Fumigation as Marks of his own Malice, and the injured Doctor's Confusion. The Chevalier resents the Insult. He challenges *Dove*, and a Duel is at Hand.

CHAP. VIII.

It is to be hoped, in the next Episode, that the Reader's Breath and Patience will not fail him, as he is like to dance through a Masquerade of very motley Adventures, and some considerable Duration.

The Adventures in the Inn.

IT happened that some young Officers, on their March to *Cork*, were bating at the Inn when the Dispute arose. These sparkish Heroes, under Pretence of calming, kindled up the Quarrel. They divided into Parties, and ranged themselves into mock Battalia, for two were *Doves*, and two were *Taylors*.

They played the Part so well, that an Exciseman and an honest Parson thought they meant to tilt in Earnest, and went upon their Knees to beg for Peace, but Things were gone too far. The Partisans of *Dove* had wrought his courage up to such a Height, that nothing less than Sword and Pistol could appease him. There must be Blood; for *Dove* it seems, had been a Soldier, and in his Youthful Years had fought against the *Nabobs*; the Seconds now are going to Logger-heads about the Choice of Weapons.

The Doctor seemed still a Friend to Peace; but *Dove* had hectored and behaved so rude, that his Spirit could not brook it; Death before Dishonour; so fight he would.

The

The Landlord was to charge the Piftols, in order to prevent all Appearance of the leaft foul Play.

When Things were ready, our two Principals, and their Seconds, which were four in Number, together with the honeft Landlord, marched out in Order to a Church-Yard very near the Inn.

Dove was peppered by his Paffion, and pranced and capered like a Jockey's Horfe.

The Chevalier, on the other Hand, looked more compofed than refolute ; yet he went. Once or twice he feemed to mutter, that *Dove* was not of Size for him, that is not of Confequence enough. But his Second, a dapper, little, lively Enfign, whifpered to him, That Honour was of all Sizes ; her Standard fitted every Gentleman : Which took away in Part the Doctor's Scruple. But he was heard to fay, The greateft Creature in the World, as ufeful as the Sun himfelf, to fight an old Philofopher, a Fellow that is fed by Fire, an Election-Dealer, he thought it was not right.

But, behold him at his Ground ! the Seconds now are bufy in meting out the Spaces, and fettling every Circumftance of Honour and Exactnefs.

The Tiger *Dove* was already in his Shirt, and feemed impatient for the Combat. He often viewed his Priming, and eyed at once the Chevalier from Head to Foot, who was not quite fo curious as his Foe, but rather, like *Æneas*, with Patience, pondered on the Event of Things, and now and then would weigh the Confequence. However he was there.

His Countenance, indeed, had given Way a little ; whether through Self-Love, or Motives of Humanity, left he fhould deftroy his Antagonift, or a Concern for human Kind, if he fhould drop ; whether one, or all of thefe together, had wrought that little Vacancy, that blank in his

Com-

Complexion, the courteous Reader will conjecture for himself at his best Leisure.

The Time is now important; for lo! they are left together.

The Seconds and the Landlord stand aloof. The Combatants are now upon the very Edge of Battle. A dreadful Interval was marked between, and *Dove* could hardly keep the stated Bounds

The Doctor was more observant, and did not pass the Line; when *Dove* cries out, A Pox, you Puppy, fire — *Taylor*, you are a Coward; look up, and see your Man.

That Word Coward like a Flash of Lightning, kindled all the Powder in his Blood. He views his Priming too; present he did, and after that he fired; the Smoke is quickly gone, and there stands *Dove* as stout, as safe as ever, grinning in his Fury; for lo! the Doctor's Shot had mist him.

Dove, forgetting Discipline, rushes on, in spite of all Intreaty, close to his Antagonist, and fires in the Doctor's Face The Doctor fell upon his Back; indeed his Countenance and Breast are bloody.

The Seconds now come in; they raise him up, enquire for the Wound. The Doctor still seems breathless, they wipe the Blood away; no Wound as yet appears, the Doctor still was breathless; with that the Ensign swore the fright had killed him, and asked the Landlord how he charged the Pistols? With nothing, please your Honour, but a little Chicken's Blood tied up in a Pudding.

The Doctor now recovers, looks pale, and blushes. The Laugh is very loud, yet *Dove* is blamed in Earnest. The Landlord swore he was a bloody Villain, and by Jesus he should pay for it.

However, Things were huddled up for the present, the Champions were made to shake Hands. The Seconds marched them back to Dinner;

where

where all their former Acrimony was overlaid with Laughter, Wine and Raillery.

The Bufinefs of the Battle furnifhed Hints for Pleafantry; but ftill the Landlord's Stone was in his Sleeve againft *Dove*.

He could not forgive him that Spite and Cruelty he put in Practice in the Article of Shooting, and was refolved to make him fuffer in his Turn.

The Evening is arrived and the Champions now are charged with Wit , as high as before their Piftols.

Dove, who travelled with a Doxy was the firft who broke up Company. His Dame and he are gone to go after.

The Doctor and the Officers kept the Field a little longer, and then retired in their Turn.

The Doctor feldom indulged his Drinking to Excefs. The Girls, or, as he called them, his Chicks, engroffed his chief Attention. He ever had an Eye to Bufinefs of that Kind, and was generally pretty fortunate in his Amours.

He was not idle now. The Landlord's Kindnefs for *David Dove* was ftill increafing. He prepares an Apparatus to prove his Manhood in another Way. A Cord is let down through the Cieling to an under Room, which Cord was faftened to the Centre of our Sage's Bed, beneath the Ticking to be fure To the other End which dangled in the Room below, an Apple was annexed, which Apple hovered over the Surface of a Bowl of Water that ftood upon a Table in the middle of the Chamber The Apple and the Water were very near each other, and ready at every Touch to play at Bobbing-*Joan*.

Thus ftood the Apparatus waiting for the Experiment, whilft another Cord, in a dexterous Hand, was ready to execute a different Office over Head. It was not hanging; the other Ex-

treme

Complexion, the courteous Reader will conjecture for himfelf at his beft Leifure.

The Time is now important; for lo! they are left together

The Seconds and the Landlord ftand aloof. The Combatants are now upon the very Edge of Battle. A dreadful Interval was marked between, and *Dove* could hardly keep the ftated Bounds

The Doctor was more obfervant, and did not pafs the Line; when *Dove* cries out, A Pox, you Puppy, fire — *Taylor*, you are a Coward; look up, and fee your Man.

That Word Coward like a Flafh of Lightning, kindled all the Powder in his Blood. He views his Priming too; prefent he did, and after that he fired; the Smoke is quickly gone, and there ftands *Dove* as ftout, as fafe as ever, grinning in his Fury; for lo! the Doctor's Shot had mift him.

Dove, forgetting Difcipline, rufhes on, in fpite of all Intreaty, clofe to his Antagonift, and fires in the Doctor's Face The Doctor fell upon his Back; indeed his Countenance and Breaft are bloody.

The Seconds now come in; they raife him up, enquire for the Wound. The Doctor ftill feems breathlefs, they wipe the Blood away; no Wound as yet appears; the Doctor ftill was breathlefs, with that the Enfign fwore the fright had killed him, and afked the Landlord how he charged the Piftols? With nothing, pleafe your Honour, but a little Chicken's Blood tied up in a Pudding.

The Doctor now recovers, looks pale, and blufhes. The Laugh is very loud, yet *Dove* is blamed in Earneft. The Landlord fwore he was a bloody Villain, and by Jefus he fhould pay for it.

However, Things were huddled up for the prefent, the Champions were made to fhake Hands. The Seconds marched them back to Dinner; where

where all their former Acrimony was overlaid with Laughter, Wine and Raillery.

The Bufinefs of the Battle furnifhed Hints for Pleafantry; but ftill the Landlord's ftone was in his Sleeve againft *Dove*.

He could not forgive him that Spite and Cruelty he put in Practice in the Article of Shooting, and was refolved to make him fuffer in his Turn.

The Evening is arrived and the Champions now are charged with Wir , as high as before their Piftols.

Dove, who travelled with a Doxy was the firft who broke up Company His Dame and he are gone to go after.

The Doctor and the Officers kept the Field a little longer, and then retired in their Turn.

The Doctor feldom indulged his Drinking to Excefs.   The Girls, or, as he called them, his Chicks, engroffed his chief Attention.   He ever had an Eye to Bufinefs of that Kind, and was generally pretty fortunate in his Amours.

He was not idle now.   The Landlord's Kindnefs for *David Dove* was ftill increafing.   He prepares an Apparatus to prove his Manhood in another Way.   A Cord is let down through the Cieling to an under Room, which Cord was faftened to the Centre of our Sage's Bed, beneath the Ticking to be fure.   To the other End which dangled in the Room below, an Apple was annexed, which Apple hovered over the Surface of a Bowl of Water that ftood upon a Table in the middle of the Chamber The Apple and the Water were very near each other, and ready at every Touch to play at Bobbing-*Joan*.

Thus ftood the Apparatus waiting for the Experiment, whilft another Cord, in a dexterous Hand, was ready to execute a different Office over Head. It was not hanging; the other Ex-

treme

treme the Toe, and not the Neck was then in Danger The Philofopher, at length and his fair Dame are lodged, but the Fumes of Wine, for fhe had drank her Quota as well as *Dove*, had rendered both the Votaries of *Morpheus* on the fudden.

Bacchus had conquered the Queen of foft Defires, and both thefe Lovers lay fnoring in a State of deep Abftraction ; when, in this unfeeling Interval, the Snare is faftened on, and *David Jemmy Dove*'s Toe is compaffed with a Cord, which Cord, without an Apple, is let down through another Hole, and hangs in a perpendicular Sufpenfe with its flender Collegue

The Centinels are fixed ; they watch the Apple and the Bowl, but no Alarm is given.   The Guard is now relieved   A Servant-Maid has got the Charge, and lo ! the Crifis is at Hand.   The long expected Signal begins to nibble at the Bowl, the Apple dips itfelf a little, and narrow Circles ftir the peaceful Lake.

A fudden Paufe enfues, and fomething like a State of Anarchy prevails.   An Interval of neither this nor that, but rather what refembles both ; like a Man who labours to regain his Stirrup, but is not able yet to mount.   The Girl upon the Guard however gueffed that fomething was a coming.

She clapped her Hands and rung the Bell, when *Sally* from the Cellar came rufhing in, and held in either Hand a Bottle full of Claret.   She faw the Image of the Spot, fhe fprings, fhe runs, fhe cries out, Mafter ! Sir ! the Apple and the Bowl.   And in her Ecftafy and Hurry fhe ftruck the Bottles, as fhe went, together : the Pavement floats with Gore

Her Mafter cries, You Bitch the Bottles. *Sally* anfwers the Apple is in the Bowl, Sir. He fees

and

and believes—he saw the Circles spread, the Apple sink and rise—he pulled the other Cord with all his Might. And now the Bowl was in Confusion. A Noise is heard, and Oaths and Groans succeed. Here, *Polly*, do you pull, pull tight; I'll go and call the Doctor; he shall hear the Villain groan.

Away he runs, and *Polly* still keeps pulling; for she hated *Dove*, the House was never the better for him. He brought his Goods along with him: But the Doctor still was furnished in the Family. So she kept pulling. But now the Devil himself was over Head, and all his Works. Rascal, Villain, Blunderbuss, and Bitch, and Whore, and shoot him dead, and Damn ye all, was echoed through the Stair Case, Passage, Kitchen, Yard and Stables.

The Doctor in his Shirt scampers like a Fury, followed by the Landlord.

The young Commanders, not better covered, follow both; and *Dove*, with a Hanger in his Hand and the Cordage at his Heels, as naked as the best of them, came roaring in the Rear, and limped about, and damn'd and sunk, and called for Satisfaction: the Servants sluiced him, for the Pump was near.

The Officers had seized the Landlord. The Doctor mounts the Hayloft; the Hostler is his Friend. The Officers, now bursting with implicit Fun, would fain appease the Landlord. They beg, they pray to know the Cause: For God's sake, Mr. *Heeny*, what is the Matter? This is a *Christmas* Trick indeed; why in such a rage with *Taylor?* Oh Gentlemen, the Villain and my Niece—Damnation seize his Duel—but I'll have his Life for it.

They lug the Landlord into the House; the Servants knew the Thing before; they bring the

Chevalier

Chevalier his Cloaths, and his Equipage is ready *Dove*, half drowned in the Scuffle, and naked as at first, begs for Heaven's fake the Doctor would take him up and fave his Life. Up he mounts, the Cord still fastened to his Toe, away the Doctor drove, and *Dove* was at his Side, shivering with Cold and Anger; but *Taylor* gave him his Surtout, and closed the Chaise about him; they journey on and leave the fatal Inn behind them.

They now are seven Miles nearer *Cork* then when they mounted first: They whip and drive, and lo! another Inn is visible.

They soon alight and march into the Kitchen; where they meet a Dozen young Gentlemen equipped for their Horses, and ready for a Hunting-match. They no sooner saw the Chevalier and his Fellow-Traveller, than they cracked their Whips, fet up the Whoop and Holoo, and swore a Stag had come to challenge them; for *Dove*'s Appearance had fet the Joke on Foot; they skelp him with their Lashes.

And here the Doctor's Malice, or Revenge, call it which you will, began to work. This was the Time he thought to fettle all his old Accounts with *Dove*.

He begged the Gentlemen would spare him; that he was an unhappy Person, a Lunatic, and had many dreadful Intervals. In one of his Fits, fays he, the poor Gentleman broke loose from his Keepers, and, naked as he was, came running to the *White-Heart-Inn* just as I was mounting into my Carriage. He knew me. And finding him tractable, I ventured to take him up, in Hopes that Dr. *Caffedy* in this Neighbourhood, who is famous for such Cures, might do him good. The Cause of his Mishap was Jealousy.

At

At this *Dove* began to fwear and damn, and tell his Story.

But the Doctor begged they would affift to give him the Cold Bath, or, in lieu of that, to drench him well under the Pump, efpecially his Head. Gentlemen, I know fomething of this Affair myfelf. There is nothing in his Cafe can ferve him more for the prefent

So faid, fo done. To the Pump he is carried ; and there, out of meer Charity, they labour for his Good.

The Patient foams. and roars, and tears, but all in vain. The Procefs ftill goes forward. The Gentlemen relieve each other at the Pump.

The Patient now is overcome with Cold He is carried back into the Kitchen wrapt up in Blankets ; and when recovered he is, by the Doctor's Orders, largely let Blood at both his Arms. The Doctor did the Surgeon's Part himfelf Now put him into Bed, fays he, and I will pay three Men for watching him till Dr. *Caffedy* is come.

Poor *Dove*, by this Time, was altogether paffive. He is put to bed, and wanted not a Guard to watch him ; but a Guard there was.

The Doctor and the Gentlemen grow very great together They drink fome mulled Champaign. The Doctor is difcovered, and careffed with Marks of high Efteem.

One of the young Bloods told him, He hoped that it was a lucky Meeting ; that he was refolved, in a Day or two, to have waited upon him at *Dublin*, with a young Lady a Sifter of his, who had a Blemifh upon her Eye. But, Sir, fince you are here, that Journey is prevented. My Houfe is but two Miles off ; and if you will do us the Pleafure to fhare in our Diverfion of To-day, in the Evening you fhall fee my Sifter.

The

The Doctor thanked him; said he was not furnished with a Hunter; nor indeed was he Horse-
man enough for that spirited Recreation.

To this they all cried out, He should have both
a sober and a good Horse. They were sure of excellent Sport, and he need not run into any the
least Danger. He might stand upon a Hill, or take
the easiest short Cuts he liked.

Aye, aye, says one of them, Lord, the Doctor
need only to ride in Company with Sir *Goddart*,
and then you know, Gentlemen, he's safe enough.
Sir *Goddart*, Sir, is my Grandfather, a very serious
old Gentleman, that about some fifty Years ago
could lead the Troop himself; but now, poor Man,
he is content with looking on at a Distance. He
loves, like a good Sportsman, the Sound of the
Horn. A Servant always waits upon him. Stick
close to him, and all is well

The Doctor in a Moment is equipped, and out
they sally with Sir *Goddart* in the Center.

It was not Day-light yet. In half an Hour's
Time they come to the Ground appointed.

The Doctor is in very high Spirits. His Horse
he thinks a good one. He wishes eagerly for the
Chace; when lo! a hell sh Roar, in a Minute, and
the Fox are set a-foot together.

The Doctor's Head is dizzy. He catches hold
of the Mane in one Hand, and the Bridle in the
other, and still he keeps his Eye upon Sir *Goddart*,
who scampers off among the foremost.

The Doctor's Horse, without consulting him,
hurried on as fast, turned as he turned, and leaped
as Sir *Goddart*'s leaped. Never was Emulation at a
higher Contest than between these two hot, am-
bitious Hunters.

The Servant still kept near the Doctor, who now
cried out for Help. No sooner had he spoke, than
whip he springs through a quickset Hedge, and
leaves

eaves his Hat and Wig behind him.   His Face is forely fcratched.   His Perfon got the Start of his Horfe, and was pitched fome Yards beyond his Head; but received no other Damage than being well foufed in Mud and Dirt; for the Ground was foft on which he fell.

He turns upon his Back; he clears his Mouth and Eyes that now were full of Filth.   He feels his Limbs and Ribs, and every Thing was fafe: And now he fits upon his Breach.   He ftares about, and wonders where he is, for the Fall had ftunned his Intellect a little.

The Footman now comes up with the Doctor's Hat, Wig, and Horfe, and whoops and holloos in his Ears, and fwears Sir *Goddard* and the Fox are got a Mile a head.

I wifh they were both in Hell, fays the Doctor.

Oh, my Friend,. the greateft Man in the World.

Why, that old Rafcal rides like the Devil.   I'll no more of the Hunt.   Friend, help me to my Horfe, and lead me back again.   Sir *Goddart* is a Guide for *Lucifer*.   Oh damn his Crack of the Whip for me.

'To which the Footman anfwered, What, Sir! Sportfman's Luck, no more; you only found a. Spur; for Shame, let us on; the Gentlemen will expect you.   Sir *Goddart* now is weary; follow me, and never, fear; your Honour is concerned, Sir.

At this the Doctor rein'd the reftif Steed about: The Footman gallops off like Fury: The Chevalier's defpotic Palfry purfued as faft.   The Doctor. is again attached to both his Sides · His Legs are growing to them: His Hands are faftened to the. Mane.   The Bridle and the Stirrups are left at large; and Filth, and Splafh, and Gravel, fly like. Shot.

Shot about him. The Hounds are at a Lofs a few Minutes The Huntfman and Sir *Goddart* are bufy at the Fault: and the Doctor, blinded and out of Breath, is juft upon the Point to join them, when off again in full Cry they fcour.

The Doctor's Horfe again purfues Sir *Goddart.* And now the Strife was mighty; two Hedges and a five-barred Gate are paffed. The Doctor, ftrange to tell, ftill keeps his Saddle. Sir *Goddart,* in the laft Attempt, is tumbled down. His Girt gave way His Horfe ftands near him. And lo! the Doctor's Horfe for once obeys the Bit. He lights with all the Speed he could, and ran to the old Knight's Affiftance, who lay with the Saddle on his Breaft and Face, and kicked and fprawled as- if for Life. The Chevalier ftoops down and catches him in both his Arms, with, Sir, I hope you are not hurt Indeed you rid too faft.

The old Gentleman, inftead of thanking, chattered, fputtered out, and bit him by the Nofe. The Doctor fwears and ftarts, with Zounds and Blood, what's here? a Monkey? and with his loaded Whip returned the laft Civility.

Reader, believe it as you will, it feems in very Truth Sir *Goddart* was no other than an old overgrown Baboon, which the Landlord ufed to drefs up and tie upon an Horfe, in order to regale fuch Sportfmen as the Doctor.

He feels his Nofe, and returns again his Thanks. The Footman is approaching The Doctor ftorms and ftamps, holding ftill his Nofe. You party-coloured Rafcal, what Affront is this? you Scoundrel, King of the Rainbow, you lick-plate Villain. Sir *Goddart* toffed about, and bitten by the Nofe! Your Mafter, Sirrah, is a greater Scrub than you. Perdition to Sir *Goddart,* my Nofe is fpoiled for ever—No more Intrigues—O *Dove,* thou art revenged—*Dove* fhall fee my foul Difgrace, bitten

through

through and through, the Shape is spoiled for ever; the Pox, no doubt.—And in his Rage he interlines a Stamp or two upon the Monkey. The Footman cries out Murder, the Baboon brought him many a Shilling. He seizes on the Doctor; the Doctor gets him down, and rushes to Sir *Goddart's* Horse, his own was at a Distance, he mounts, and sees the Huntsman and the Hunters coming towards him at full Speed. He claps Spurs, and turns the Horse's Head towards the Inn. He left his Hat and Wig behind him · they fell off in the Squabble with the Foot-m ..

The Huntsman is arrived, and sees the Monkey gasping He clapped his Hands and cries out Murder too; for he had lost a Friend.

In a Word, the whole Crew, the Hounds and all, follow, now in full Cry, the Doctor, who drives he knows not where. But the Horse knew better, and took the shortest Way to the Inn. The poor Chevalier clings close, and holds with both his Hands the Mare, excepting now-and-then the one he borrowed to rub his Nose with The Dogs are near upon him, and all the Crew cry out to stop the Murderer.

Reader, image to yourself his Figure, fastened as he was to the Horse's Neck and Sides, without either Hat or Wig, his Nose, quite bitten through and bleeding, rough-cast besides from Head to Foot.

In this weather-beaten Plight he enters the Inn-Yard, with all the Hell-Hounds at his Heels; and what was worse than all, *Dove,* exulting, beheld it from the Window, and gave three feeble Chears to welcome him.

And now the Farce is drawing to a Crisis. The Hunters were divided in their Sentiments. Some said, the Doctor was to blame; but the major Part pretended much Compassion, and said, the

Landlord

Landlord was a Rascal for putting such a Trick upon any Gentleman.

In a Word, all Parties are at last good Friends. The Monkey too grew better. They passed the Day and Night like Bucks indeed. *Dove* and the Doctor shake Hands the second Time, and forgive all. *Dove*'s Cloaths are brought him. The Doctor, with a Patch upon his Nose, and he set out for *Cork* together in the Morning.

C H A P. IX.

A meer Resting-Place, with some little Entertainment.

AT *Cork* he carries all before him. The Cures he wrought, which to those People looked more like Miracles than any human Process, made him the Idol of the Populace. Nor was he less admired by People of Fashion. He returns to *Dublin* in *November,* finds it very brilliant, being Parliament Winter. He arrives in the Evening, appears in one of the Boxes at the Theatre, shining like a Constellation. The Audience clap him at his Coming-in, and the Ladies curtesy; not the Viceroy himself was more distinguished.

His Friend *Dick Eagle* is about this Time let down a Peg or two. A Gentleman of real Merit in the Profession of Portrait-Painting, had driven him quite out of Fashion; so *Dicky* turned Player. At which Business he was worse, if possible, than at scrawling Pictures. Yet acting, together with his other Trade of Pimping, kept for awhile his Chin above Water. He was often with the Doctor, and did him twenty little Offices of seeming Friendship, but inwardly he envied him; though the Doctor was not his Rival in any Thing but Fame.

He

He could not bear to fee him fhine over him, and was refolved to bring him down to his own dirty Level, if poffible.

The Doctor loved a Wench, and *Dicky* knew it.

One *Sunday* Morning he waits upon the Chevalier, and tells him, he has appointed two handfome Country Laffes to meet him at the *Yellow Lion* in *College-Green*, where, fays he, Doctor, you fhall have your Choice, or both, if you like it. Agreed, quoth the Doctor.

Accordingly he came, and met the Damfels. They travel up Stairs together, the Doctor and the Ladies, whilft *Dicky* did Duty at the Door. The Hoftefs had her Cue from *Dick*; fhe had her Part to act. Upon Notice given fhe travels up the Stairs, and in her Hands fhe bore a Spit with a Leg of Mutton well nigh roafted thereupon; fhe enters at a Point of Time that happened to be critical; fhe cries out, Rogue and Whore! and lays upon the proftrate Doctor the Warmth and Weight of all her Mutton—The Gravy deluged now his Face and Linen—He ftarts, he ftares, he holds up both his Hands,—his Drapery is difordered. She repeats her Oaths and Blows. The Doctor takes to Flight, embarraffed as he was about the Hams, and to the Street he hobbled, but left his Coat, his Waiftcoat, Wig and Hat behind him; his under Drapery ftill difordered, he hobbles on, all fmeared with Gravy; the Mutton at every Blow ftill burfting about his Ears.

O fatal Unities of Time and Place! It was one o'Clock on *Sunday* in the Afternoon, and lo! the Congregation is rufhing from out the *Round Church* Door, juft as the Doctor and his Kitchen Fury were paffing by: Yea, all the People, nay the Parfon too beheld it.

Haplefs

Haplefs Doctor! where was then thy Diamond Crofs and Ring, thy fpangling Coat, and all the Apparatus of a noble Gentleman? The Ladies fcream, they run back to Church again. The Parfon hides him in the Pulpit. The Mob came round. The Beggars fcramble up the Mutton. The Hoftefs now is out of Breath: She falls upon her Face, by miffing of a Blow, with Arms out-ftretched, the Spit was ftretched out further.

The Doctor now is raging mad. An Oyfter-Wench reftored his Galligafkins, and fmiled upon the Frolick; when lo! a Gentleman, a Senator, for he reprefents the City, beheld the Doctor's evil Plight. He came between, and with his Prefence awed the Tumult. The Rabble now are fcattered. In his Coach he took him, took him naked as he was and fanguined over.

Notwithftanding his Misfortune, the Senator efteemed his Merit, and loved him as a Man. The Fumigation was not worfe than this. But oh! much worfe was yet to come. Grief on Grief! his Wife and Son, that very Inftant, are arrived from *Scotland*. What a Climax of Diftrefs!

Dublin was no more a Place of Safety. No Safety for *Jack Taylor* there. He meditates the Continent *Dick Eagle*, in a hackney Coach, brings him this News, and with it brings the Doctor's Drapery, who bid him ftrait go back and countermand her Journey. I muft not fee her; let her again on Ship-board; on Ship board put her and her Son. O damn your Country Wenches, *Dicky*. *Dick* thou haft undone me.

Dicky now was burfting inwardly at the Joke, but wore a Countenance of feeming Sorrow, more in Fraud than Friendfhip. The Villain wept with Triumph, and promifed never more to pimp.

He waits on the Doctor's Lady, perfuades her to re-imbark, affures her her Hufband will meet her

in

'n the Morning, and fail with her to *England:* Which indeed he did. But firſt he puts on Board a ſtately Horſe, that with his Trappings coſt him near two hundred Pounds. He brought beſides with him two Footmen in blue Liveries turned up with Silver, a large beautiful young Wolf Dog that coſt him twenty Guineas, together with ſome Rarities from the Giant's Cauſeway, as a Preſent for the royal Society.

They hoiſt Sale, meet a Gale of Wind, are driven by a Storm upon the Coaſt of *Wales,* where they landed in much Danger of their Lives.

CHAP. X.

This Chapter is of a mixed Conſtruction. A tragic-comic Tale. The Scene ſtill ſhifting.

THE Chevalier leaves his Wife at the firſt Town he comes to, and ſets out Poſt for *London.*

He had not journeyed far, before he encountered a handſome rich Widow, to whom he made the warmeſt Tenders of his Love ; told her, he was a Widower, had only one Child, whoſe Nurſe he permitted to go in his Name, as ſhe was young and obliged to travel with him.

His Confidence, his fine Perſon, and genteel Addreſs, ſoon gained Ground upon the Widow's Affections. She complies But the Affair had now reached his Wife's Notice, who haſtened to the Town where the Widow and he were, found Means to produce the Certificate of her Marriage to the abuſed Widow. But the Doctor, through meer Dint of native Bronze and artful Contrivance, defeated his Wife's honeſt Attempt, and baffled her ſpiritual Authority, confirmed at the ſame Time

the

the Widow in her firſt Sentiments, aſſured his Wife
that the Affair was a meer Galamaufry, and giving
her a Kiſs, together with five Guineas, and his
Picture ſet in Gold, he adviſed her by all Means to go
back to the Town from whence ſhe came, which
was *Carmarthen* ; and being in Haſte to diſpatch
her, he hired a Guide to take her the neareſt
Way.

We cannot ſuppoſe, that he, a meer Stranger in
that Country, could be acquainted with the Road
through which he was to travel   Whether the
Widow, in her Care for Mrs. *Taylor*'s Safety and
quick Return, had adviſed this Step, will alſo be a
Queſtion not ſo well cleared up as the Reader could
wiſh.   Be that as it may, the Road ſhe was put into was known to be impracticable by all the Neighbourhood, eſpecially at that Seaſon of the Year,
on Account of the Tide, which roſe to ſuch a dangerous Height between two Hills, that it made all
Paſſage that Way quite deſperate.

The miſguided Lady ſoon found her Danger.
The Water ruſhing in and riſing ſo high in an In-
ſtant alarmed her much, and as it happened not
quite too late.

The Guide was making off with all the Speed
he could.   But ſhe cried out to him, to come and
adjuſt ſomething about her Stirrup ; which the
Fellow did.   She being a Woman of ſtrong Spirits,
ſeized him by the Collar, and ſaid, if he did not
ſtay and help her out, he ſhould drown with her.
Upon this they quit their Horſes, and with great
Toil and Danger they clambered up the Cliff, and
got ſafe to *Carmarthen* to the great Aſtoniſhment of
every Perſon in that Town.

Mean while the Doctor ſets out with the Widow,
whom he ſettled as his Wife in an Apothecary's
Houſe in *Bloomeſbury-Square*.   His real Wife remained ſome little Time in *Wales*, and then followed

lowed him to Town ; where, in Order to fatisfy herfelf concerning the *Welch* Widow, fhe gets acquainted with the Apothecary's Wife, tells her who fhe is, and by her Connivance dines with the Widow. In the Height of Dinner, the Poftman brings a Letter from the Doctor. The Widow rofe up in great Tranfports to read it ; yet Mrs. *Taylor* had fuch Command of her Paffion, that fhe feemed to look on with much Indifference, till Tea was over, then took her Leave with gieat Temper ; nor was fhe, by the Widow, in the leaft fufpected.

Upon the Doctor's Arrival, the Apothecary gave him Warning to quit his Lodgings, telling him his real Wife had been there ; he would have no fuch Doings under his Roof. The Doctor, without taking Leave of any Mortal, fets out for *France,* with the Widow, immediately.

But firft, by Way of mcer Convenience, he drew, as the Widow's Hufband, fifteen hundred Pounds out of the Funds.

He arrives at *Paris :* And though he feemed to love this Woman even to Madnefs, yet through a ftrange Caprice of Soul, he would not let her call him Hufband. No truly, like the Patriarch of old, fhe muft be thought his Sifter.

With her Cafh he fets up at once a flaming Chariot with fix dapper Greys, and Servants in rich Liveries, and looked as grand as an Embaffador. But Fortune, like other Ladies of Fafhion, delights in Variety : She feemed to make our Doctor her Topic of Diverfion. His Scene was always fhifting ; and every Movement gave fome new Appeai ance.

CHAP.

CHAP. XI.

A new and severe Test of our Hero's Courage and Patience.

A *French* Gentleman, handsome as the Doctor and full as amorous, happened to cast a wishing Eye at the Widow. She returned his Overtures with Interest. The *Frenchman* was coming up apace Sword in Hand. The Widow was about to beat a Parley. The Doctor saw and trembled. Duels were his mortal Aversion And Things were now so much embarrassed, that he must either declare, look on, or fight. Declare he did, and swore she was his lawful Wife. The *Frenchman* retired from the Siege in Form. But whether Matters ended there or not, is still a Mystery, and, like many others, is indeed of little Consequence.

The Doctor now was at his vertic Point of Glory, blazing as he travelled. Two whole Years he dazzled the Faculty at *Paris*, kept the best Company, and got much Money.

But alas! an unlucky Accident made it a little convenient for a while, at least, that he should break fresh Ground.

A young Lady, of one of the first Houses in *England*, who lived in a noble Family near *Paris*, had got a Dimness in one of her Eyes, the brightest else in *Europe*. The Chevalier was called, who with his wonted Felicity soon dispelled the envious Cloud. He was richly rewarded for this Piece of Work, became a Favourite in the Family, where he passed some very pleasing Hours.

The Lady's Gratitude and familiar Carriage so natural to the *French*, for she was educated there, overset, it seems, the Doctor's Prudence. Something
thing

thing had poſſeſſed him with a ſtrange Notion, that the young Lady's Civilities, ſeaſoned by Gratitude and Kindneſs to her Benefactor, for ſo ſhe eſteemed the Chevalier to be; I ſay, this Appearance, free from all *Gothic* Ceremony and rude Reſerve, flattered this Son of *Æſculapius* to make ſome ſtrange Concluſions in his own Favour; for his fine Perſon was ever whiſpering to his Vanity.

In ſhort, he uſed to walk by Moon-light with this delightful Beauty in a Grove that ſtood near the Houſe. His Frenzy ſtill grew ſtronger. He ſaw her through a Medium which Vanity had caſt before his Sight. Heightened by Deſire, in this Illuſion, he fancied ſhe was going to fee him with her Perſon. He perverted every Circumſtance. Her Looks, her Words, were all Conviction. He reſolves to ſnatch the happy Minute, proceeds *vi & armis* to practiſe upon his Patient a new Operation. She ſtrikes him on the Face — ſhe cries for Help — the Servants are at Hand, and oh! Diſgrace to Knighthood, the Chevalier was forced to travel through the Horſe-pond, with many Baſtinado's on his outward Man.

Paris, after this, was again too narrow. He ſcours back to *London* with ſome Thouſands in his Pocket. He takes a Houſe in *Suffolk-Street* at near £ 200 a Year Rent, with Offices for ſeveral Carriages, and Stables for a double Set of Horſes, tho' then content with a Pair of hackney Kephals faſtened to a ſplendid Crane-necked Chariot.

At his firſt Appearance in this Equipage, a very ſtriking Circumſtance was taken Notice of, and it was this: The Doctor, that great Dealer in the viſual Ray, had in all his 'Train but a ſingle Eye, which happened to be the Coachman's Property, for the Horſes were both of them ſtone blind.

Here

Here he orders two large Rooms to be laid into one, which he intends for his Library, having, he said, brought together a numerous Collection of the beſt choſen Books in every Language and Science.

His Landlord, being a Man of Taſte and Letters, was licking his Lips at the Thoughts of being regaled by the Doctor's Library.

The expected Morning is come, when two Porters from the Tower are arrived, one leading a Horſe with a Sack Load of Books upon his Back; the other keeping the learned Cargo in its Place. The Sack is opened, and lo! the Doctor's Library, *viz* Various Editions in ſeveral Languages of the renowned *Don Quixote*; *Gil Blas*, *Swift's Tale of the Tub*, in *French*; *Bunyan's Pilgrim's Progreſs*, three Volumes of *Caſſandra*; *England's Converſion and Reformation compared*; *Dr. Anthony Gavan's Maſter-Key to Popery*; *Hobbes's Leviathan*, looſe in the Binding; the Hiſtory of *Montelion*, Knight of the Oracle; *Grey's Love-Letters*; *Ray's Wonders of God in the Creation*; *A Preſent from a Parſon's Wife in the Highlands of Scotland*; *The ſolemn League and Covenant*, *Sacheverel's Trial*; *Wycherly's Country Wife*; *Cauſin's Holy Court*, *Milton* and *Don Bellianis* of *Greece*: Such was the Doctor's Collection, which make an elegant and full Appearance in the two large Rooms prepared to receive it. And never was there more Space allotted for leſs Matter, except in the *Vacuum Boylearu*, or perhaps in the Doctor's own *Pericranium*, which ſome Wags have compared to his Library.

When the Houſe was furniſhed, as indeed it ſoon was in a very elegant Manner, he placed the Widow in it as Miſtreſs of the whole.

CHAP.

CHAP. XII.

A Christmas Frolic.

AND now he fastens four more Rozinantes to his Carr, with two Servants in rich Liveries behind it ; with which, and his Valet on Horse-back, he sets out for the Place of his Nativity — Has the Appearance of Grandeur in every thing about him, except his Coachman, who served as a moral Contrast to the gaudy Parts of his Retinue, and did the Office of a Death's Head at a *Roman* Feast ; he served to shew how perishable all world-ly Grandeur is. But indeed he served further ; he was a striking Mark of his Master's motley Cha-racter. His upper Weeds were much worn out ; his Elbows took the Air ; you would think his Breeches were beleaguered, for there a mighty Breach appeared ; he lacked Boots and an upper Tunic, though it then was Winter.

Previous to the Doctor's setting out, he filled the *Norfolk* News-Papers with Paragraphs of his own vast Importance. Never was the Art of Puffing displayed to such Perfection. He sends Letters to his Fellow-Citizens and Brethren, being himself a Free-Mason, inviting them to meet him , which indeed they did in great Numbers, and in their best Appearance. He also employed People to set the Bells a ringing as soon as he entered the City-Gates.

In this triumphant Manner did he drive up to his Mother's little Shop, bringing with him such Quan-tities of rich Cloaths, that he was forced to hire the next House as a Ward-Robe, where they were laid out and exposed to the public View.

Here he meets with his Wife and Son, who had lived at *Norwich* during his Residence in *France*.

He alfo met with his old Friend *Tabitha* the Quaker's Widow, with whom he paft an Evening, and cut again her Corns. He flies about two Days together like a Meteor, and then returns to *London* with his Wife and Son. He puts the Boy to School at *Kenfington*, and places his Wife, *fans Ceremonie*, in the fame Houfe with the Widow, where the Wife was her conftant Chum, in order to hinder the Doctor from being fo.

Thus Affairs went on for fome Time. The Doctor made a bright Appearance. The Cures he performed ; the Concourfe of Nobility and Gentry who daily crowded to fee them, brought him great Reputation and Confequence. The very Faculty, in fpight of Prejudice, could not forbear giving him his juft Applaufe.

C H A P. XIII.

Which confifts partly of nice Reflexions, and partly of odd Adventures.

A Gentleman of Rank, whofe Son the Doctor had reftored to Sight, procured him, as a Mark of his good Will, to be made Oculift to the King.

With this Feather in his Cup, and his own folid Merit, were he half as prudent as he was prodigal, he might have continued his Copper-gilt Chariot with fix Dapples, and ten thoufand Pounds in his Pocket. But alas ! his chimerical Fondnefs for Show led him into a Million of inchanted Caftles. Oftentation was the Idol that undid him : And, what is ftrange, he grew more and more in Love with thefe Fairy Vifions, as he advanced in Years. He never was happy, but when, like a Comet, he was ftared upon. The Character he affumed was
that

that of the marvellous. He imitated, nay invented every romantic Extravagance. The Epic and the Grand were the Chevalier's natural Stile.

He was no less magnificent within, than without Doors. Nothing but Grandeur muſt come near his Table. Courſes ſerved up in all the Maſquerade of Luxury, where Nature was inviſible, created Diſhes, coſtly Wines, Muſic, and all the Madneſs of a *Roman* Feaſt were his higheſt Triumph. And yet, to make this Prodigy ſtill more prodigious, no Mortal was ever leſs anxious about his Palate than the Doctor. A broiled Blade-bone of Mutton without a Cloth; a Cruſt and a little Salt; ſtanding at ſome Dreſſer in his Boots and Riding-Coat, made up a thouſand Ortolans.

He was an Epicure in Idea only. His Table, like his Cloathing; was meant for others to gaze at more than his own Enjoyment. He would be viſible — Nay the very blind muſt ſee him. But that indeed was his true Ambition.

His wild Oeconomy ſent him Abroad once more. He ſets out for *Paris,* hoping that Time had defaced the Memory of the fatal Horſe-pond.

He left the Widow at a Lodging in *Chelſea,* and his Wife and Son in the Houſe at *Suffolk-Street,* where they remained till the Landlord had ſeized upon the Goods for Rent. This melancholy Event happened a ſhort Time after his Departure, they not having wherewith to ſubſiſt on in *England,* were forced, by Neceſſity, to follow him into *France.*

The Doctor is at *Paris,* where Ambition in a new Shape has ſet herſelf before him. A Shape indeed without a Subſtance. He turns Author in an evil Hour, as if he had not Misfortunes enough before. He neglects his Patients. The bodily Eye was now, forſooth, a meer mechanic Organ, much too coarſe for his Inſpection. The intellectual Sight, the Eye of the Soul, was now his favourite Object.

Ho

He writes a Supplement to the learned Bishop of *Cloyne*'s Book, to prove that there was nothing but Mind in the Universe. The intellectual Eye he now proposed to couch, and purge all Mists from thence. But there he reckoned wrong. A thousand Quacks to one were there against him. His Patients of this Class received no Benefit. They are as blind as ever. His Finances fall short. He gets into Debt, meditates a new Province, but first he places his Son in the *College du Placis* facing the *Sorbonne*, leaves his Wife at a Hotel, and sets out in the Night for the City of *Bourdeaux*; though he had it in his Power to make as great a Figure in *Paris*, as he did at *London*.

He also leaves behind him one of his Chicks, as he calls them; she was a beautiful young Damsel, whom he had inveigled from a *French* Nobleman, which cost him Woe.

In this Article he stands accused of violating a little the Laws of Hospitality. He was daily at his Lordship's Table, and received a thousand Favours at his Hand. But Love conquers all. He settled Matters so that his beautiful Chick was let down the Wall in a Basket from her Window, whilst the Doctor stood below with open Arms to catch her. 'Twas in a Garden, where unluckily a *Danish* Dog was upon the Watch, who took the Alarm, and rushed upon the Doctor just as the Basket was dropping into his Lap. His Valet, assisting in that very Moment, had half his Leg torn away. The Doctor's Throat escaped by a Miracle, for the furious Animal seized him by the Collar. The wounded Valet, however, with his Rapier dispatched the animal. The Lady lay sprawling all this while. But the Doctor, with the Loss of half his Waistcoat and Coat Skirt, made off with his Prize, who having the Keys of the Garden Door, let herself and Lover into the Street; where they quickly

got

got to Shelter, and left the poor Valet to shift for himself in the best Manner he could.

This smuggled Piece of Beauty the Doctor kept for his private Use, till Money falling short, he left her also in the Lurch.

The Nobleman after his Departure, had her taken up, and put into a House of Correction, as the Custom of the Country is, where during a Woman's cohabiting with a Man, as much Fidelity is expected from her, as is if she was really his Wife. In this House they are shorn of their Hair, that of the Head I mean. They are cloathed in coarse Weeds, and go through a painful Process by the Way of Penance; a Regimen too severe for her delicate Constitution She could not support it, and died of these Hardships in less than four Months.

C H A P. XIV.

In this Article of our History, something of the marvellous may appear, together with something of the small.

THE Doctor is now at *Bourdeaux*. He goes on with great Success He has an Account that his Wife is dangerously ill at *Paris*. He reports that she is really dead, puts on Mourning, and in a little Time pays his Court to the Mayor's Daughter of the Town; who, dazled by his Appearance and Popularity, began to listen with some Attention to his Proposal; yet his Discretion caused him to send to *Paris*, to learn from thence if the Doctor told him the Truth; but he is assured, that the Chevalier's Lady is not only living, but perfectly well recovered.

He

He lets the Doctor into this very Secret, not without some Menaces; which so alarmed him, that he scampers over the *Pyrenæan* Mountains, and arrives at *Madrid:* Where, in his unguarded Zeal, he talks loosely of religious Matters. Besides there were found upon him some heretical Books. He finds his Danger, and flies for Refuge to Sir *Benjamin Keene,* our then Embassador at the Court of *Spain*; by whose Assistance he makes his Escape to *Portugal.*

Just as he was entering upon the Frontiers of that Kingdom, in a Post-Chaise attended by two Servants, between the Hours of eleven and twelve at Night, he was attacked by six armed Men, who were in Pursuit of a Murderer. They take him to be the Man. The Doctor not having *Spanish* enough to explain himself, and suspecting he was pursued as a Champion of the Church of *England,* defended himself with great Courage and Zeal. He resolved to fall a Martyr, rather than submit. He fought so long, that both his Servants were killed and one of his Horses. He received some Shots in his Cloaths. At last, finding that Superstition was like to prevail, he, with much Reluctance, yielded himself up, and was dragged by them to a Garrison at four Miles Distance; when, upon producing his Passport, the Mistake came out; a little too late indeed.

He arrives at *Queensbury,* a University in *Portugal,* where the Art of restoring Sight was very little known. Here he dissects the Eye, and gave public Lectures upon the Method of treating its Diseases; which he did with so much Judgment and Ingenuity, that till he put his Theory into Practice, they looked upon his Dissertation as mere Fiction.

Though our Doctor was then in Distress, yet his Merit and Success established his Reputation to such a Degree, that he obtained Letters from the University to the Court of *Portugal*, recommending him in the strongest Terms. Where, in a few Months, he had the Honour to be made a Knight of the Order of Christ.

Here for three whole Years together, he lived like a Nobleman. In which Time, among many others of smaller Note, he restored to Sight the Viceroy of *Brazil*; for which Feat he got, to use his own Words, a Hat full of Gold. But his evil Genius was here again at his Elbow, and pushed him once more into that eccentric Path, which led him so often out of the straight Road.

He intrigues with a very handsome young Lady, the Wife of an old rich Physician, who was pleased to entertain the highest Esteem for the Doctor; and, contrary to the Custom of that Country, gave him free Admittance into his Family, where he sometimes met his Wife. The Doctor a good Judge of the Eye, soon saw something in the Lady's Look which promised an Adventure.

In short, he amused himself agreeably with this Lady the best Part of a whole Year. Nay, he had gone so far as to advising the Packing up of Jewels and other Trifles of great Value, which, he told her, would be useful in a Journey, for they were to set out for *England* together. Nay, she had promised him to turn *Protestant:* For that was a Point the Doctor never forgot to cultivate in his Dealings with either *Jews* or *Papists* of the fair Sex. His Zeal for the Church of *England* kept equal Pace with his Passions of Gallantry. And he could reckon as many Proselytes as Mistresses. But the Doctor, like Captain *Mackheath*, could as soon be satisfied with one Woman as one Guinea.

He is caught at the Reverend Fathers the *Jesuit's* Church, by a Lady, who happened to adjust

E 4   her

her Veil in his View, which gave some Glimpse of a Bosom white as Snow. The Veil in *Portugal* speaks the Language of all Countries. The Doctor takes the Hint, commences Admirer, is led by the Lady into a very elegant Exchange of Civilities.

This relieved the Sameness of his Collation at the old Doctor's. The Variety gave new Life and Spirits to his whole Deportment. He appears more brilliant and engaging. He feels a fresh Ardour kindle in his Bosom to the Religion in which he was educated.

The Spirit of his Mission stirred strongly in him. And now the Mistress of a *Popish* Archbishop is to be brought over to the Communion of the established Church of *England*; for such is the Lady, who now felt the force of his Argumentations. His Reasons, she thought, were much stronger than those of the Archbishop. He made deeper Impressions upon her, and she gave Way very quickly to all his Motives. Such was the Measure of his Talent in the Art of Persuasion.

But the female Hypocrite above-mentioned hath Notice of his Progress in this spiritual Warfare. She lays up Vengeance for him; and in his next Visit she receives him with great Shew of Affection, tells him, she has got a Glass of the finest White-Wine in all *Spain*, which he must give his Opinion of. She fills to him, and he drinks two or three Bumpers with Glee; said he never tasted any thing so excellent. But, Madam, says he, all your Favours are the richest upon Earth.

Traitor! says she, I am revenged—you have drunk the most powerful Poison in the World—you have not an hour to live—The Archbishop's Mistress, Traitor! At these Words she flew out of the Room, with a thousand Furies in her Face.

The

The Doctor now sat more like a Figure of Ice, than a breathing Mortal. His whole Life came rushing into his View. His Conscience, startled from its Slumber, stares him frightfully in the Face; a thousand Terrors, the past, the present, and the future, are all before him. He beats his Forehead, plucks off his Diamond Cross, and flings it to the Floor. He stamps, he raves, he roars, he runs to his House, without hearing or seeing any thing in his Way. He cries for Help.

Here he meets the Chaplain of the *English* Factory, and another Gentleman, his Friend, to whom he roars aloud for Help. They are amazed. He cries out, Poison! Poison! *Taylor* is no more, my Friends—I die, I die—*Taylor* is cut short, and the World is lessened. I feel it boil among my Bowels. My Stomach is on Fire. A Puke, a Puke, a Puke! My Cross, my Diamond Cross, and all my Titles for a Puke. I confess I am a Sinner—'tis now no Time—O yes, I have a Wife and Son at *Paris*—Sir, assist me; I have blinded many—caught, caught in my own accursed Snare—this Fire consumes me—Yes, I believe it all, the Creed, the Trinity. O give me the hot Water, drench me to the Muzzle. *San grado* now assist me—it works up and down—the Poison works me stronger—Sir *Hans Sloan* shall have my Instruments—My Art who can inherit?—My darling Son—O I've wronged my Family—My Pulse is sinking—Yes, I've wronged my Family—this dreadful Woman—The Rattle-Snake is not more fatal—I have made some Converts, Sir; will that atone?—

Now the Apothecary pours in sweet Oils. He is drenched unmercifully, and brought so low, that he gives up all Thoughts of Life. He begs the Parson's Help, and thinks of the other World in earnest.

He

He makes his Will in the Intervals of the Cloſe-Stool and the Bowl. His Candle now was burning at both Ends. He expects every Moment it will go out. I bequeath my Works to the College of Phyſicians: Ah, no, ſays he, I'll leave them to my darling Son. I'll leave him all my Papers. They'll make him ſome Amends The Materials for writing my Life, under my own Hand, he ſhall have them all. My Croſs is gone for ever O read the departing Prayer! I ſink, I die——The Poiſon maſters all my Vitals——No human Art can conquer it——O lay me on the Bed. My Reaſon too begins to totter.

. Here he is put into Bed. The Parſon gives him Abſolution. His Friends all kneel around. The laſt Prayer is read. He dozes in a kind of Stupefaction His Eyes are cloſed, but ſtill he breathes.

'Tis now beyond the Hour of Midnight, when lo! a grave Perſon, in the Habit of the Faculty, enters the Room, deſires to ſee the Chevalier. He feels his Pulſe, ſhakes his Head, and ſeems much concerned He offers him a Cordial, but alas! he utters not a Word. The Voice he ſeemed to notice, and he opened by Degrees his Eyes. The Phyſician offers him again the Cordial, but in vain.

At length, his Mouth is opened, and down he pours the Draught. 'Twas like Sir *Walter Raleigh's*. He feels a Flaſh of Lightning dart through all his Inwards. His Colour kindles by Degrees. And now he ſhews ſome Signs of Life. Nay, he ſpeaks, and aſks what ſaving Angel had thus relieved him. He takes more Cordial. He ſtill grows better, and he gazes on his Doctor. The Diamond Croſs he feels within his Hand; and ſomething then is whiſpered in his Ear.

At this he raised himself a little, looks wild about him, and cries out, Reverend Sir, I am not dead; take back the Absolution, they will never sign it over Head — O my charming Chicken, in her Husband's Cloaths too, what, no Poison then, but *Spanish* White-Wine! oh, it was a damn'd Dose — I'll no more of the Bishop's Mistress — Yes, I'm better, O my sweet *Physician* !— It was a devilish Dose indeed. Mr. *Simpson*, this my charming Chicken, my darling Convert, and my Diamond, are both come back. The lucky Minute ! I have them both again — recall the Absolution — Ah, it was a little cruel, but I mend apace — She will read her Recantation now — We will strait for *England*; you've got the Diamonds and the Money Aye, aye, we will strait for *England*. Mr. *Simpson*, you'll befriend us — A Proselyte is a precious Thing ! — Yes, we will strait set out — Another Gulp will set me on my Legs — Oh such a rasping Dose, it had like to send me packing, the greatest Creature in the World.

The Parson was in amaze. But the Lady, in her Husband's Breeches, assured him, all was true; that she gave him nothing but a Glass of Wine to drink She was sorry they had puked and purged him so, but, says she, it will serve him both for Physic and Philosophy; it will correct his Humours and his Morals too. We must be gone. If my Husband should suspect, we are undone for ever.

The Chevalier was much recovered. The Chaplain advised him not to stir that Night; said, the Lady might read her Recantation in *England* to more Advantage; he would give them all the Assistance in his Power; advised them to keep close, till they had heard again from him, which would be in the Evening after To-morrow.

The

The Chevalier expreſſed his Thanks, begged of him once more to take back the Abſolution, revoked his Will, declared his whole Behaviour was but acting a Part, he meant nothing ſerious, and begged of the Chaplain as a Man of Honour, to report him ſo, leſt it ſhould hurt his Reputation as a Gentleman, which was a Thing he valued much more than his Life.

The Chaplain ſtaréd at him; but promiſed to obey, and to get Things ready againſt the Time appointed, and bid them both good Night.

CHAP. XV.

A Scene of Tenderneſs and Sincerity will here furniſh out a Contraſt to our Hero's general Character.

THE Lady now expreſſed great Sorrow for the Harſhneſs of her Medicine. She apprehended it ſeems, that it might have no friendly Effect upon her Night's Entertainment; ſo ſhe made her Choice to ſit up and cheriſh the Doctor with Cordials and with Kindneſs, till he was in ſome Degree reſtored to his priſtine Faculties. They ſettle the Plan of their intended Flight. Her Huſband, ſhe ſaid, knew nothing at all of her. She had taken her Opportunity in his Abſence; and (notwithſtanding his Falſhood) ready to go round the World with him. She hoped Mr *Simpſon* would be punctual, for every Hour was an Age.

The Doctor endeavoured to convince her in the beſt Manner he could, that his Affection for her had not loſt all its original Energy, and was but partly ruined; he felt his Vigour and Integrity return. Facts are convincing Things; and the Doctor was not idle. In this Interval of Dread

and

and Joy, they paſt their horrid, happy Moments in expecting ardently the Chaplain, ſtill ſtretched upon the Tenter-Hooks of Hope and Fear. A Condition of Mind which none can deſcribe or imagine, but thoſe who have felt it.

The important Minute was now approaching near, and Expectation went abroad to meet it. The Rumbling of a Coach alarms them. They ſtart with Rapture at the Sound, and vowed the Chaplain was an Angel. They ſpring to meet him. But oh ! what Language can deſcribe their Terror ! They meet the Holy Office at the Door, the Midnight-Coach, and all the black Tribunal. The Inquiſition now has ſeized them. This Thunder-Clap was worſe than all his Pukings.

The Chevalier, the Lady in Diſguiſe, his Books and Papers, are all ſeized and carried off to Priſon, to the dreadful Priſon.

He is accuſed of being a *Jew*; and a fearful Proceſs is begun

Two Brothers of the Faculty, in their Envy of his Merit, did him this Kindneſs. He ſaw before him a Proſpect truly terrible. They put him to the Torture in a Manner not unlike the Fumigation, and full as dreadful.

Here the Chevalier ſoon felt the Difference between this infernal Juriſdiction, where Innocence itſelf is often criminal, and a Nation, whoſe civil Polity is but mere Humanity exerciſed by Truth and Reaſon, where Law is Liberty, and Subjection perfect Freedom ; where Religion is the Handmaid of Virtue, to dreſs her out in all the Ornaments of Moderation, Humility, and every ſocial and ſublime Attractive.

In this horrid Extremity, he found a Paſſage to a noble Lord, the then ambaſſador from *England* at the Court of *Portugal*, a Character illuſtrious all over *Europe*, whoſe Reſolution is equal to his

Huma-

Humanity. Through his Lordship's kind Application and powerful Influence, the Doctor is at last inlarged. When nothing less than Providence, in the Person of his noble Benefactor, could have wrought his Delivery, which was brought about rather by a Connivance of the Court of *Portugal*, than through any legal and open Process.

He escapes in the Night. His fair Friend, out of Petticoats attends him in his Retreat. Nor had he Leisure to bid the Bishop's Mistress one soft Farewell. He felt some tender Pains on her Account, for he lost a Proselyte; but his good Intention he hoped might be accepted. The Inquisition cancelled half his Passion; but his Zeal was still invincible. Nay, he gained a tenfold Force from his Adversity. He vowed revenge like *Hanribal*, and would sacrifice a thousand Nuns as Victims to his injured Mother the Church of *England*, and his own Resentment. He determined to go and make Reprisals, whilst aught of Man remained in him.

He is now upon his Journey; his fair Fellow-Traveller and he. They are mounted upon Post-Horses, and leave behind them, in their Haste, all their Apparel, except the Suits they had on, some Jewels and things of Value they had secured. But alas! the Poor Lady was so disordered, by the Fatigue of her Journey, that she had a Fever on the third Day after their setting out. It increased continually. Her delicate Frame was not able to sustain it; and though she fell ill at a Place the most unpromising in her Situation, yet she wanted no Assistance that Art or Kindness could administer, for the Parish-Priest was himself a good Physician. He was always with her; and not only him, but a Gentleman of the Faculty, the worthy Father's Brother, happened to be then upon a Visit with him.

The

The poor Lady grew worse and worse. And the Chevalier, to do him Justice, was pierced to the very Soul with Sorrow. Her affectionate Generosity and Friendship were working at his Heart. He sees her sinking to the Grave on his Account.

In short, all Hopes of Recovery are given over. The wounded Chevalier feels an additional Pang. The Thoughts of her dying a *Papist*, after all the Pains he had taken in her Conversion, recoiled grievously upon his Virtue. O! it was a two fold, a goading Affliction; but Necessity must be obeyed

She is new upon the Verge of a Delirium. She gives the Chevalier her Jewels; and, with Tears and dying Tenderness, she begs him to be gone, and leave her to the Priest's Humanity, who would see her decently interred At this her Understanding quite failed, and she said no more to be understood.

The Doctor waited till she was quite senseless; and then, taking silent Leave with a sorrowful Heart, he posted off with all Speed.

He knew her Sex must soon be discovered, and the Danger which must follow. He therefore travelled Night and Day, till he came to a convenient Port, where he took Shipping; and after a very dangerous Voyage, landed safe at last at *Falmouth*.

End of the First VOLUME.

Lightning Source UK Ltd.
Milton Keynes UK
UKHW052044150223
417096UK00021B/301